MONEY ME CRAZY!

A PRESCRIPTION FOR MONEY SANITY

TED McLYMAN

Money Makes Me Crazy
229 Fury's Ferry Road, Suite 141
Augusta, GA 30907
Phone: 706-860-2490
www.myapexx.com
Email: info@myapexx.com

The Money Makes Me Crazy and the icon "financial stickman" are registered trademarks of Apexx Behavioral Solutions Group. All rights reserved. Except for brief excerpts for review purposes, no part of this book may be reproduced or used in any form without written permission from the publisher.

ISBN 978-0-9830353-0-5
© 2010 Ted McLyman
Published in association with Larry Carpenter of www.christianbookservices.com
Cover Design: Debbie Sheppard
Author Photo: Rob Forbes
Printed in Canada
First Edition 2010
1 2 3 4 5 6 7 8 9 10
2010 10 08

CONTENTS

FOREWORD

Ted McLyman and I had been traveling in parallel universes without knowing that our paths would eventually cross and our ways of thinking about the world would converge on the issue of money. My career as an Industrial/Organizational Psychologist, coach, and consultant has been dedicated to the idea that the choices we make on a daily basis can get filtered through all of the experiences of our life. When we can recognize what may be clogging our filter and affecting our choices, we are able to clear out the negative influences from the past and we are equipped to make informed choices that take us in more powerful and resourceful directions.

I thought I had it all figured out. But I was left with the nagging question—"If I'm so smart, why am I so broke?" As it turns out, Ted helped me to understand that I was not alone in failing to realize that our primitive brains are great at keeping us alive, but not so good at helping us to manage our finances. And while we may have wisdom in many other areas of our lives, we are actually hardwired to be stupid about money!

I always say, "when we know better, we do better." One of the most impactful learnings for me from Ted's teaching is the fact that my financial condition is shaped by the same influences that shape the other areas of my life. *(Duh! Now why couldn't I see that?)* Our biases and limiting beliefs create a theme in our lives that shapes the way we approach relationships, our work, *and* our finances. Our fears and insecurities not only prevent us from establishing a confident perspective and healthy interpersonal and work relationships, they also serve as barriers that block healthy decisions about money and investing.

I am optimistic and confident about my future, and I intend to live a long time and to enjoy my old age. I also consider myself to be a philanthropist and community volunteer. But here is what I have had to learn. In order to live out my life as I have defined it, I need money. Plain and simple. In order to fund the causes that are important to me, I need resources!

Coming to this realization was quite an "Aha" moment for me, because I was raised to believe that the desire to become wealthy was not an admirable ambition. This book and Ted's teachings have led me to a healthy perspective of money as a tool that needs to be managed to serve the purposes for which I intend, and not as an evil addiction that I can expect to rule my life.

The process of stepping back and recognizing our current biased thinking leads us to the point of being able to let go of stored negative emotions and limiting beliefs. We can then reframe our perspectives to adopt a more resourceful mindset that will propel us into the future we desire.

My best advice to you is that you take time to use this book to help you take a look into the mirror. Then step back and consider what insight you gain about yourself—*you really aren't stupid, you know!* Get in touch with your dreams and be confident about the kind of future you want to create for yourself and others. And most importantly, use that insight to fuel BETTER CHOICES in the future!

Faye Hargrove, PhD
CEO, The Hargrove Group
and Author of the book, BETTER CHOICES

INTRODUCTION

I bet when it comes to money, we are a lot alike. Have you ever run into a store to buy milk and bread, only to end up spending a small fortune? Do you have a favorite store? Why do you like it? Do you have friends and family who think you are irrational with your money? Do you wish these same people would approach money just like you do? You know you get money right—and you can prove it! Are you overwhelmed by all your buying choices and the 24/7 assault on your senses to spend your money? Finally, are you convinced that the rules of money have changed—but no one had the courtesy to fill you in on this little secret? If it helps, you, I, and a few million other people think and feel the same way.

I wrote this little book to help you work through these questions. The book is a quick and easy read—no charts, no graphs, no math, and no product recommendation. It is not an academic review of the current literature and research on how we make our money choices. There are a number of excellent books that cover the subject in detail if you need more information. Think of this book as your survival guide to the mall—or wherever you make your money choices.

The theme is simple and straightforward. Humans are not wired to work well with money. The behaviors that kept us alive in the forest can kill us at the mall.

- Money decisions are always emotional.
- Everyone has a unique money temperament.
- Our money strategies should match our money temperament.
- The old financial industry is all about products—features and benefits.
- The new financial industry is all about behavior—temperament and strategy.
- Know your money temperament and manage your behavior to create wealth.

This book is about *you and your money and not a book about "money."* I want to help you better understand how you think and feel about money. Once you understand how and why you make your money choices, I believe you will make better money choices. I've been working with people and their money for years. That's what I do. Money does make us crazy. You are human. And humans aren't wired to be very good with money. Once you understand this—that your money behavior is emotional and very human—you can start to better understand how and why you spend your money the way you do. In fact, "money crazy" seems to be our natural state. If any of this is of interest or a concern to you, read on. If not, spend on—but you will have to deal with your money behavior eventually.

The book is divided into two parts. Part I is about money behavior—why you make money choices the way you do. Part II is about managing your money behavior—*The Money Behavior System.* I've tried to use the best laboratory available to demonstrate all this—The Mall. I could not think of a better place to talk about what we Americans do best—spend money. In Part II you'll meet "A. Pexx." Think of A. Pexx as your "Sherpa money guide" who resides in your subconscious and helps you make better money choices. I hope to help you find your inner "A. Pexx," and by doing so, to help you make better money decisions. A. Pexx will help introduce and explain the Money Behavior System.

OVERVIEW

Part I: You are Human, Get Over It

- Chapter 1: Crazy Money, Stupid Money. Lays out the challenges we humans face daily with our money choices
- Chapter 2: Surprise—You are Not Very Good with Money. Why understanding your human nature and how you think and feel about money will help you make better money choices
- Chapter 3: It's All About You and Your Money Beliefs. Why understanding your money belief system is critical to better money choices
- Chapter 4: The Rules Have Changed. Why what you know about money might not work in today's rapidly changing economy

Part II: The Money Behavior System

- Chapter 5: Your Money Values. Why knowing what is most important to you in your life is critical to making better money choices
- Chapter 6: Your Money Temperament. Why knowing how you think and feel about money will help you make better money choices
- Chapter 7: Your Money Knowledge. Why knowing how you take in and process information is critical to your money success
- Chapter 8: Your Money Strategy. Why having a "big picture" money plan will help you achieve your critical money value

- Chapter 9: Your Money Action. Why a plan without action is worse than no plan at all
- Chapter 10: Now I Get It. Know yourself to make better money choices

Most people seem to either not understand or choose not to understand how they make decisions about money. The social and economic impact of this is huge—it results in everything from lost opportunities to stress to individual and corporate bankruptcy. Fixing this will benefit everyone. I hope to motivate you to look more closely at how you make your money decisions. Using the insights from this book and a little work, you can make better money choices in the future.

I wrote this book because:

- I'm tired of trying to fix money mistakes that should never have been made in the first place—and being blamed when I can't fix them. I've sat with far too many people who look good, smell good, and are broke. Having a lot of things you don't need and can't afford is not wealth. Children are great—I have two—but sometimes saying "no" is okay. Buying your child a new BMW for his/her sixteenth birthday does not make any sense if your financial house is not in order (six months' savings, debt under control, a retirement plan, insurance, etc.). Waiting until you are in your 50s to start saving for retirement is not a good idea either. Calling me to talk about long-term care insurance for your mom after you learn she has onset Alzheimer's really limits your options—sorry, it's too late.

- You need to know how to work with financial professionals like me. If you knew what I know about what I do, you would not try to do what I do. Good financial advice is not difficult to find. What's difficult is fitting the advice, the products, and the services to you and then actually getting you to follow the advice. Sounds easy. It's not. If two PhDs with Nobel Prizes in economics can get it wrong (look up "Long-Term Global Management"), what makes you think you can get it right? I was at the trading desk of the largest mutual fund company in the world a few years back talking with one of their money pros (advanced degrees, years of experience, access to CEOs and policy makers, very SMART person) the very day she missed a major market downturn. She just got it wrong. She eventually lost her job because of it. This is hard even for the pros.

- Financial services professionals who work directly with the public giving advice and selling products and services also need this book. We need to do a better job of understanding how our clients think and feel about money—their money temperament. Our industry focuses far too much on products and services, capturing assets, beating the market, and getting paid. We think we know our clients, we think we have good client relationships, and we think we are pretty good at what we do for them. Unfortunately, this is not always true. Generally, our industry does not consider money behavior when working with clients. Risk tolerance is not the same as money behavior. Thinking about client behavior is a relatively new aspect of the financial services industry. I believe this will grow in importance in the future. We have to consider behavior—both our clients' and our own—to serve our clients well. It is time to learn something about money behavior.

You need to understand how you think and feel about money. Your money temperament is all about you. You are unique; therefore, your money temperament is unique. There is no incorrect money temperament. You simply need to know what it is and how it influences your money decisions. Since this is all about you, we'll help you explore what makes you "you" with regard to money. What are your values? (We'll help you understand the difference between Values and values.) What is important to you? How do you make choices?

To make better money decisions, you need to know a little about the financial services industry. Not the entire multi-trillion-dollar finance industry, just the personal services piece. The industry is changing rapidly. The rules have changed, and you need to know what they are. The way we in the industry do business today is different than how we worked just a few years ago. How we work in the future will be different than how we work today. Change is a constant in this industry.

The prescription for making better money decisions is: 1) accept that you are human and will always act human, 2) know who you are and your money temperament, and 3) understand and apply the *Money Behavior System*. This system assumes that in today's economy everyone is "self-employed." You are in the business of "YOU." You have to look at yourself as the CEO of your own business. It does not matter where you work or what you do. You are now self-employed—you are the boss. Your only guarantee is the opportunity to work. Your only security is your level of performance. Even with great opportunities and great performance, you might not make it—our economy can be a bit tough at times.

The *Money Behavior System* is just the tool you need. This system, if used correctly, will help you make better money decisions. The System is simple in concept but powerful in execution. It asks you to address five very simple questions:

- What are your money values?
- What is your money temperament—how do you think and feel about money?
- What is your money knowledge—how do you process information and what do you know about money?
- What is your money strategy—what is your master plan for financial success?
- What is your money action plan—how do you put your plan into place?

I said this was pretty simple; but like everything else, it may take a little time and effort to accomplish. However, when you answer these questions you will have a much better understanding of how you think and feel about money. This should make you much more comfortable with your money decisions. This also means you should be much more effective and efficient in spending your money and be able to work better with the money professionals you choose to hire. This is good for everyone.

If money makes you crazy—and sometimes stupid—this is the prescription you need.

PART I:

HUMAN MONEY BEHAVIOR

This book assumes that 1) you are human, and 2) money makes you crazy. I also assume that you don't like your current condition. In Part I, we'll talk about why money makes us crazy as we address certain concepts:

- We are human, and the behavior that kept us alive in the forest might kill us at the mall.
- We are not very good with money.
- It's all about us and our money beliefs.
- The rules of money have changed.

Money is the common denominator of modern life. If you hope to do better with your money, you need to know something about why you behave the way you do with your money.

CHAPTER 1

CRAZY MONEY, STUPID MONEY

H as this ever happened to you? Things are going great then out of nowhere you realize that you are going to run out of money before you run out of month? When you check your bank balance you wonder where all your money went. And when you try to remember what you bought you don't have a clue. Or, over a weekend when you have nothing better to do you decide to inventory of all the things you own. And at some point when you are knee deep in all your stuff you figure out that your money priorities might need to be adjusted. If this is you, has ever been you, or you know someone like this—read on. You might find out why money, at times, makes you crazy and sometimes stupid.

Everyone I know has a money story—crazy purchase, lost opportunity, paying too much for something, and so forth. Myself, I've had a conflicted relationship with money for as long as I can remember. My love-hate relationship with money exists because I am human. And we humans aren't very good with money—sorry. As hard as I try, my emotional, irrational brain keeps getting in the way of my thinking, rational brain. That's why I have a house that is too big, a car that cost too much, and a garage full of stuff I don't need but can't seem to part with. I have squandered both time and money in pursuit of happiness—money makes me crazy.

Since you're human, I bet you are a lot like me. I suspect you have a list of dubious money choices you'd like to do over. Think about this for a few seconds. Have you ever bought anything on impulse? Do you always make a list before you shop? How's your budget going? Is your retirement plan on track? Are you always rational with your money? Does everyone you know feel and think about money the way you do? If not, why not? Here's the deal. I assume you are reading this book because you aren't always happy with your money decisions. Could my money affirmation be your money affirmation? Money makes everyone nuts from time to time. That's a given. What is important is how you deal with it.

I've been working with people and money all of my life. In the chapters that follow, I'm going to share with you my observations and best practices about people and money in order to help you get your arms around how you think and feel about money. If you believe everything you see and hear about money—from your brother-in-law to the "talking heads" on cable television—making good money decisions is easy. All you need is the right product, service, and/or technique and you can do it—all by yourself. I wish it were so easy. If it were, everyone would be rich and you would not have to read this book. Just look around. Lots of people, from every walk of life, don't seem to get it when it comes to money. "Normal" seems to be having money issues and not the other way around. Why? Because we all face four significant money challenges:

1. We are human. Our human nature gets in the way of making good money decisions.

2. We don't understand how money choices are made or how our unique money temperament influences our money choices.

3. We believe the common wisdom that we are rational decision-makers with our money and that all we have to do to be successful is select, own, and manage the right products and services.

4. The rules of money have changed. The rules that may have worked for your parents or grandparents might not work for you.

So why do you need another personal finance book? Good question. There are thousands of books out there—too many. Here's a secret I learned a few years ago. All of the books, web sites, and "expert" advice on personal finance will do you no good until you first know how you think and feel about money. Money sanity is about behavior. If you want to manage your money well you must manage your spending behavior and know how you make your money choices.

Unfortunately, most of the personal finance information and guidance I've seen seems to use a "one-size-fits-all" approach. It's good stuff, but it's presented like it's the Holy Grail. The challenge for you is to figure out if the recommended approach is suited to your money temperament. If it isn't, you just get frustrated. For example, how many books and articles have you read about budgeting? They all say about the same thing. Set some goals. Live within your means. Track your income and expenses... This is all well and good, if you are wired to do the detailed work necessary to collect the data and build your budget. If you don't like collecting and entering data, you aren't going to do this drill for very long. Your temperament trumps whatever you want to do. That's why you are really good at collecting data for a few days. Then you miss a few days, the drills get tedious, and soon you drop the whole program—you have to love human nature. Some people are wired to do this (a lot of them are in the financial services industry), but not everyone. The question is, "Are you?"

Down in the trenches where we spend our money, we know money decisions are emotional and that we all should be more rational with our money. We try hard to do the right thing, but it's so difficult and the consequences of bad choices can be catastrophic. We also know that the "cookie-cutter approach" to money doesn't always work, and at times it makes things more complicated. Here's the bad news—managing money is difficult. But there is good news—it's not impossible.

In the chapters that follow I want to help you look at managing money from a different perspective. I want you to see money through your eyes based on what you feel and think about money. I want to help you better understand your unique relationship with money—your individual money values and temperament. I want to help you improve your money knowledge. This will then help you develop your unique money strategy and action plan based on your money values and temperament. It's that simple. Your prescription for money sanity is to know yourself and manage your money behavior.

Managing money well is important. The challenge is to make a good decision with the available information you have, based on your situation. Unfortunately, life happens; you do sometimes get it wrong and you seldom get a "do over." We all know managing money is hard work—at least emotionally. However, it is not rocket science. It all comes down to four simple things:

1. Time. You don't have as much time as you think, and once it is gone you can't get it back. You have to manage your time wisely. Time gives you leverage and can make you money.

2. Money. You do need money to make money. You have more money than you think. You have to make choices. You need to really look at what is important about money to you. This is an allocation problem—where to spend your scarce dollars. The good news is, there are lots of ways to get money if you put your mind to it. Always invest in yourself first.

3. Rate of Return. This is simply all the financial products and services in the financial markets that "pay" you as either an owner or a lender. Here's the critical point: as an individual you can only select how you want to be paid (the financial products you want to own or lend). The market determines how much you get paid. The key is to own the right mix of stuff and not chase the rate of return.

4. Behavior. Wealth and financial success are all about your behavior. Manage your behavior and you can control your money destiny. Financial success is not about financial products and services. Financial success is about knowing and accepting how you feel and think about money and having a strategy and plan that works for you.

Of the four, behavior is the most critical element of financial success. Since behavior is so important to your success, you need a place where you can observe and study money behavior. I assume you aren't a behavioral economist with a research facility and library, so we'll have to make do with what you have locally in order to study money behavior. The best place in the world to do this is your local mall. This is where money behavior all comes together. And it's great fun to just watch.

THE MALL

Here is a scenario to help you understand the feeling-thinking tug-of-war that is going on inside your head every time you have to make a choice with your money. You are the prime character in this story. Play along. It will give you a window to peer into your spending brain. We'll come back to your mall throughout the book to help identify and explain money behavior.

This quick trip to "The Mall" happens daily all over the country. The location and players are different, but the behaviors are on-target. Role-play as you read the passage. Try to focus on the spending behavior. Ask yourself if you have ever had a similar shopping experience or know someone who has.

Suppose a friend you ride to work with asks if you mind stopping by The Mall on the way home from work to look at a new line of high-end shoes that are on sale at "The Big Expensive Department Store." You know your friend has an important presentation later in the week. A new pair of shoes sounds like a good idea to you. You agree, but only if it is a quick "in and out" trip. You do not need anything and wanted to save your money for a big concert later in the month.

You arrive at The Mall at about 5:30. The Mall is an upscale development serving mostly professionals who work in the area. Parking is a mess due to construction. Therefore, you have to park at the other end of the building from The Department Store. You both agree that this will be a quick trip and head off for the entrance.

Upon entering, a delightful man greets you and informs you that today is "Construction Madness Sale Day." He gives you and your friend a scratch-off coupon good only for today. You perk up and get a little excited about the prospect of saving some money on some good stuff. You scratch off your coupon and learn that you have "won" a 25 percent discount on all purchases. Your friend's discount is only 15 percent—you smile and clutch the coupon. Even though you had not planned to buy anything, you keep the coupon because you never know what you might find "on sale."

The two of you look at each other, high-five, and head to *The Department Store*—way at the other end of the mall. Immediately you sense the quality and "class" of *The Mall*. Everything seems "right": the colors, the light, the noise level, the music, and the smells. Everyone you see looks successful and prosperous.

Along the way, you stop at a number of stores. You remember that you are saving for the concert and you do not buy anything (only looking and taking mental notes). The two of you finally reach *The Department Store* (your friend is not as self-disciplined as you and bought a "few" great finds on the way) and head to the shoe department.

You leave your friend and begin exploring *The Mall*. You have not spent any money but you keep thinking about your coupon and hate to walk away from the discount. You could give the coupon to your friend, but, "It's mine." The very nice greeter gave it to you, not your friend.

You again remind yourself that you are not there to buy—you are only looking. Then out of the corner of your eye, you see something special. A brand new, limited edition, super-shiny, first-person-you-know-to-own, state-of-the-art "THING." (This is all about you. What does the "THING" mean to you?) You simply have to own one. Score: Mall 1, You 0.

You have been hearing great things about the "THING" for months. The advance material from the website raved about how great the "THING" is. All the expert reviews were awesome. Just wait until your friends see the "THING." In addition, with your discount coupon you will save a bundle.

You give the clerk your credit card and the coupon. She congratulates you for your purchase. You are now one of the first to own "one." You think to yourself how smart you are to buy the "THING" now, with the coupon. You think to yourself how much you are saving on shipping and that you will not have to wait for delivery. Life is good!

You rejoin your friend—who has bought two pairs of shoes and a suit (of course, they were on "Sale"). You share your story about buying the "THING" and receive accolades for the wisdom of your purchase. You both agree that you were smart to shop The Mall. You could not have "saved" as much somewhere else.

You and your friend decide to head back to the car. It is now 7:00 and you are hungry, so you stop at the food court for dinner. This affords you time to read the "THING" quick-start manual and ogle over your purchases. You also take the opportunity to text a few friends to tell them about your good fortune. They all agree that you are having a good day. After dinner, you pick up a few small things—a 25 percent coupon is a terrible thing to waste—and head home.

At the end of the month, you receive your credit-card statement. You notice that the interest rate is higher than last month and the balance is dangerously high. Upon examination, you realize that you paid a premium for the "THING." In fact, when you look at your receipt you realize that you received a 25 percent discount from the store's premium mark-up. If you had waited, you could have paid less online. You feel bad, but you think to yourself that regardless of the price, you have a first-run, limited edition "THING." Not many people can say that. Of course, that has to be worth something.

You break out the calculator and do a little math. Between the "THING," dinner, and a few extra purchases, you have busted your budget. You also realize you cannot afford to go to the concert—at least with this credit card. You look at the "THING" and sigh, "Now everyone has one." However, good fortune again shines your way. You remember that you qualify for a zero interest rate on a new credit card if you make a balance transfer. You smile and say to yourself, "Sweet! I can go to the concert after all."

Does this ring a bell with you? Can you place yourself, or someone you know, in the story? The scenario could unfold just about anywhere money choices are made—super market, website, golf shop, bank, college admissions office, financial advisor's office, and so on. In the next chapter we'll take a closer look at your trip to The Mall. For now, keep this in mind:

- Money success is between the ears.
- Know yourself first to better manage your money.
- The future is managing money behavior, not money products and services.
- At the end of the day, you will be held accountable for your money behavior.
- Good money outcomes require good money behavior.
- The Money Behavior System™, presented later in the book, is the new model for behavioral money management.

ACTION STEPS

Ask yourself, or better yet, write down your answer to each of the following questions:

1. Why does money make you crazy?
2. What was your best spending decision? Why?
3. What was your worst spending decision? Why?
4. What is one word that best captures how you feel about money?
5. What is one word that best captures how you think about money?
6. How do you make your major money decisions?
7. Does money keep you up at night? Why?
8. What would it take to give you peace of mind in your chosen life style?

9. Are you pessimistic about your financial future? Why?

10. Are you optimistic about your financial future? Why?

Let's now discuss the number one reason money drives us crazy—we are human.

CHAPTER 2

SURPRISE—YOU ARE NOT VERY GOOD WITH MONEY

THE MALL

*Y*ou are sitting at your desk at home going through your mail. You find a new credit-card statement and wonder where that came from. "Oh yeah, I remember. This is the new zero-interest-rate credit card I made a balance transfer to after my last trip to The Mall. I have to remember to pay this off. I think I read somewhere that if I don't I'll have to pay back interest." You put the statement in the "don't forget to pay" pile and open the next statement. This is from the old card. It has a zero balance—life is good. The next piece of mail is from The Department Store at The Mall. It's another scratch-off coupon. You think to yourself, "I don't think I need anything. But I wonder what my discount is?" So you do what you always do and scratch off the metallic film to see what you got. "15 percent off any purchase. Not bad." And without thinking, you put the coupon in your pocket and head out to the dry cleaners to pick up the jacket you plan to wear to the concert tonight.

The dry cleaner is in a strip mall across the street from The Mall. You pick up your jacket and pay for the cleaning with your debit card. You like debit cards because it's such a hassle to go to the bank—although you note to yourself that you seem to spend a little more freely with debit than cash. Oh well—whatever works. You notice your old credit card in your wallet—the one with the zero balance because you made the transfer—and smile. You head to your car thinking how good you are going to look tonight. When you reach in your pocket for your keys, you find the coupon from The Department Store. You think to yourself, "I'm here. Why not run in and see if they have anything I might need for tonight." So you head to The Mall—feeling good, excited about tonight, and armed with a credit card with a zero balance. Score: Mall 2, You 0.

WHAT HAPPENED AT THE MALL?

The Mall is not your friend. It conspires against you, exploits your behavior, and takes your money. There, I said it. We are weak when it comes to money. I have seen all of these behaviors in my students, my clients, my family, and myself. (I am no different than you when it comes to money. I just happen to know the technical terms for my poor spending choices and can describe the behavior.) So what happened? Two people went shopping and bought some stuff. Then you went back and did it again. Millions of people do this every day. In the grand scheme of things, nothing very exciting happened. You went shopping and made economic decisions about how best to spend your limited dollars on scarce goods and services. What is interesting is how and why you spent your money the way you did.

Classical economists assume that you are rational with your money. That when faced with a money choice—to spend or not to spend—you do a quick cost-benefit analysis in your head and select the most cost-effective choice. They contend that you make your choices in a "vacuum" without any personal or social frame of reference. To them, behavior doesn't matter.

Do you believe that? Is this how you shop? I doubt it. There is a very good chance that you have had similar spending experiences. It could have been a minor purchase or something pretty significant. It doesn't matter. Your feeling brain bought something and you were powerless to stop it. Then when your thinking brain reengaged, you didn't feel as good about your purchase.

Behavioral economists look at money decisions differently than traditional economists. The basic economic problem is the same: how to allocate scarce resources when human wants are limitless. You (or someone else) have to choose. The choice has trade-offs. When you decide to spend money on one thing, you are deciding not to spend money on something else. For example, in the story, say you had $15.00 in your pocket. You now have to make spending choices with your money. You could buy a super special hat (looking good is okay) or this book (creating wealth might be a better choice, but I have a conflict of interest). You do not have enough money to buy both. You have to choose. If you buy the book, your head goes uncovered. You might even be "un-cool." The cost of the book is really the cost of not buying the hat. Do you have it? This is what economists call an "opportunity cost."

The behavioral approach to money combines the research from economics, biology, sociology, psychology, and other disciplines on decision making. It tries to identify the context of your decisions and explain how you think and feel about your choices. It reveals how you use feelings and perception to choose, how your information about a decision might be wrong, and how your judgment might be biased or taken out of context. The result: you make bad money decisions or decisions you regret.

Unless you live alone in a cave, this probably seems obvious, especially if you are married or have a partner or children. They are likely an endless source of examples of irrational money behavior.

However, behavioral finance is a relatively new field of study. The research is just now moving from the lab to the classroom and into the market place. I believe this will eventually change how you define your relationship with money. In addition, it will in due course change the financial services industry.

Let's take a quick look at your brain's trip to the mall. You had three things going on that influenced your spending. First was the social context: how your cultural and social relationships influenced your decisions. Next, within your body you were experiencing physiological changes that influenced your decision to spend. Finally, the conflict between your feeling brain and your thinking brain sealed the deal. The bottom line is, you spent the money the minute you decided to go to the mall. Unfortunately, you did not know it. There is a lot going on when you spend money. The mall trip is a great way to highlight the money behaviors we all exhibit all the time. Here are some key points.

The Social:
- If shoes did not have a significant social value (expected level of professional dress), you would not have even gone to the mall.
- In American society, you spend money at malls. Therefore, you were preprogrammed to buy something.
- The mall had an "upscale" feel that reinforced your perception of how your peer group should look, act, and spend.
- Your friend was spending, so you did.
- We live in a "plastic" society. Very few people use cash or checks anymore. This tends to cause us to spend more.

The Physical:
- Your autonomic nervous system (control center) started taking in information.

- The design of the mall and the individual stores targeted your feeling brain. The "pleasure" areas of your brain began to react to all the stimuli and put you into a spending frame of mind.
- The sights, sounds and smells of the mall triggered past "positive" spending experiences stored in your feeling brain.
- When you saw the "THING," your brain started pumping out the "feel good" neurotransmitter dopamine.
- Dopamine makes you feel good about a purchase, even before the purchase.
- During the purchase you go into an excited state—your heart rate may elevate and your skin might flush.

The Mental:
- You placed great value on your coupon simply because you "owned" it.
- You rationalized your purchase.
- You believed all of the stories about the "THING" without checking any facts.
- You knew you had made a good purchase because you confirmed the wisdom of your purchase with others you respected as an expert, and the data you found supported your decision.
- You told yourself that you were an intelligent buyer and that you had made an informed decision, but luck put you in the mall that day.
- You were overconfident that you could resist spending any money.
- You wanted to be the first to own.
- You did not understand opportunity cost and the "cost" of money.

Money does make us a little crazy. Have you ever done anything stupid with money? Does every purchase or investment work out just as you had planned? Is your hindsight better than your foresight? Do you rationalize some of your money decisions? Have you saved enough? How's your retirement account looking? Do you have money in a zero-interest bank account while you have a high-interest-rate credit-card balance? I am sure you can add a few more questions.

As I've said before, getting money right is hard work. The pros get it wrong—a lot. So what should you do? I recommend that you concentrate on one thing first, and that is "You." You are unique. You therefore have a unique money temperament. Until you understand your temperament—how you think and feel about money—you will never have that critical "Aha" moment about your money.

You can learn about money. Money information is everywhere. You can read books and magazines, listen to the talking heads on television, attend seminars, and take a money course. None of this will help until you first come to grips with your relationship with money.

The nice thing about all this is, it really does not matter what your relationship with money is as long as you know what the relationship is. Then you can take steps that work for you based on who you are rather than following someone else's prescription for money success.

Do you follow me? This is important. There is no one else like you. You are a complex human being. You have a unique way of dealing with money. To keep your sanity with money, you must develop a "one-size-fits-*one*" approach to your financial strategy.

Be happy that some of your friends love to manage and invest money online. Some people actually have the discipline to keep a budget. You should be impressed if you meet someone who truly understands the tax code. Somewhere there might be a person who can actually explain all the benefit information you receive from your HR department. Sound money management is not difficult. Many people do get money right. So can you, if you put a little effort into learning why money makes you crazy and sometimes stupid.

The key to financial success starts with understanding and accepting how you relate to money. The rest is execution. Remember:

- You are a complex human being.
- Human nature makes money difficult.
- The way you relate to money is unique to you.
- Money success is peace of mind in your chosen lifestyle.

THE "HUMAN" TEST

If dealing with money were easy, you would not be reading this book. All your financial affairs would be in order. You would live within your means. You would have peace of mind. If money stuff were so simple, everyone would be financially okay. Just think how easy your life would be. You would:

- Be rational in all financial matters—spending only when "marginal cost equals marginal utility" (whatever that means; hint: it was in Chapter One of your Econ 101 class).
- Be fully informed and knowledgeable about all important financial matters (taxes, savings products and services, investment products and services, insurance products and services, benefit plans, retirement plans, college plans, car leases, wireless plans, all rebates, your mortgage, what Bernie Madoff did to his clients, the new Health Care bill, elder care for your parents, why gas prices are going up, estate planning, paper or plastic, if your donation to the Haitian Relief really got there, and why you should never

be late with a credit-card payment—I forgot; you only pay cash). Does your head hurt yet? There's more, but I think you get the point.

- Be unaffected by social pressure and the "consumer culture." (Try explaining this one to your teenager.)
- Have a budget and actually use it. (That means you really know what you earn, what your expenses are, and what you have left over at the end of the month.)
- Have a financial plan and in fact follow it. (I know, you did one last January.)
- Understand the difference between risk and uncertainty. (You insure against risk because you have to live with uncertainty.)
- Have financial security and peace of mind appropriate to your chosen life style. (How is that working out for you?)

Here's the real issue: humans are not "hard-wired" to work well with money. Your body and your brain conspire against you daily to make dumb spending choices. Add this to the modern consumption culture, and you have the root of your problems with money.

In the simplest of terms, you really have two brains: a feeling brain and a thinking brain. Your feeling brain does all the things necessary to keep you alive without your having to think about it—breathing, heartbeat, and so on. Your feeling brain evolved to keep the species going. It mostly deals with staying alive and passing on the genes. Your thinking brain deals with higher order things—like taxes and the small print disclaimer you see when you download software.

Your feeling brain is emotional. Your thinking brain is rational. Your feeling brain orders things from infomercials. Your thinking brain pays the bill and manages the garage sale so you can pass your stuff off to someone else's feeling brain.

FEELING BRAIN	THINKING BRAIN
• Primitive	• Modern
• Reactive	• Proactive
• Emotional	• Rational
• Multi-task	• Single task
• The default	• The exception
• Automatic	• On purpose
• Generalize	• Specialize
• Quick	• Slow
• Experience	• Prove

Your feeling brain is always the first responder in money matters. As much as you try, your initial reaction to money is emotional. The challenge is to know this, and to recognize how vulnerable your financial security is to your emotions. You need thinking-brain countermeasures to get control of your money issues.

You might be saying to yourself, "I'm not good with numbers, and I don't like to deal with money." This is the classic artist/engineer stereotype: artists can't balance a check book and an engineer can't dance. Like all stereotypes, this is not true. You can control your feeling brain and engage your thinking brain—if you want to. The trick is to identify and overcome your limiting beliefs about money and develop a money behavior strategy that fits you. That means developing a money strategy designed to complement your unique money temperament. If you are married, or have a partner, the strategy needs to complement both of your money temperaments. Now, how difficult can that be?

If you are a skeptic and do not buy into this "dual brain" stuff, try this exercise. It will demonstrate that there are things going on in your body that you cannot control. Your brain and your body are "wired" to work a certain way. As much as you try, you cannot make it do things it is not able to do. The "wiring" just is not there. So you adapt.

Try this:

- Sit in a straight back chair.
- Point the index finger of your right hand straight out and start making "6s" in the air. Simply trace the number "6" a few times with your right hand.
- Stop. I assume that was not very difficult.
- Stay seated, lift your right foot off the floor and point your toes. Now make a "clockwise" circle in the air. Simply trace a circle in a clockwise direction with your right foot.
- Stop. I assume you also mastered this task with little problem.
- Now, do both at the same time. Trace the number "6" in the air while at the same time making "clockwise" circles with your right foot.
- Stop. (If you are on an airplane, please be careful. You don't want to hit the person next to you or get the attention of the Air Marshall.)

What just happened? You made "6s" without a problem. The "clockwise" circles were easy. However, your brain is incapable of doing both at the same time. It's a "wiring" issue. The connection is just not there. You cannot will it, or hire a coach, or find a solution on the web. You are human. Humans don't make "6s" in the air while making "clockwise" circles with their right foot. The bad news is, humans do not manage money very well either. The good news is, there are solutions that will help you resolve your natural feeling/thinking brain conflict with money.

KEY POINTS

Books and courses are available that describe and analyze spending behaviors in detail. All of that is beyond the scope of this book. However, I encourage you to get into the subject matter. You will be surprised what you learn about yourself.

The key points about how and why you spend your money are:

- You are a complex human being.
- You are unique.
- You have a unique money temperament.
- Your context and culture matter.
- Your physiology matters.
- Your mental state matters.
- The behavior that kept humans alive just a few generations back does not help us much at the mall.

BECOME A PEOPLE WATCHER TO LEARN ABOUT MONEY

The best, and most fun, way to figure out why money drives you crazy is to become a people watcher. America is a consumer culture. We like to spend money. By watching how and why people spend money, you can develop an understanding about your money temperament. Here is what I want you to do:

- Become a "spending" detective. Look for the: who, what, when, where, and how money is spent.
- Listen to how people talk about money. Try to figure out how they think and feel about money.
- Take note how people spend their time. Money is part of what people find important.
- Watch and read advertising critically. Try to determine what emotions the ad is trying to target.

- Look for design elements at stores and malls that promote spending.
- Be alert for examples of "irrational" spending among your friends and co-workers, and ask yourself why you think their behavior is irrational.
- Look for examples of people making "irrational" spending choices in the media. Ask yourself why you think the spending is irrational. Then ask if you think the media presented the spending as positive or negative?
- Do all the above for your personal spending. Be aware of the context of your spending. Take note of what you think and feel when you spend your money.

Note: Please do not judge. Remember, other people are unique too. Your goal is to develop a "situational awareness" for spending. Awareness for how you, and the people around you, make spending choices. This will help you become a better consumer. Soon you will see patterns in your spending. These patterns will help you identify your money values and money temperament. Knowing your values and temperament will be the foundation for your "Money Belief Profile," which is discussed later.

Human nature gets in the way of making good money decisions. Accept the fact that your spending choices are a direct reflection of you—past and present. Modern society conspires against you to make you spend money—often on things you neither need nor can afford. You are usually a willing accomplice—even if you do not know it. This is not an excuse, only a warning. It is time to get this all under control. Managing money is hard work, but not impossible. You can get it all under control if you start now.

ACTION STEPS

Ask yourself, or better yet, write down your answer to each of the following questions:

1. How does your culture influence your spending?
2. Are you aware of the context of your spending, i.e. location, social situation, peer pressure, and design elements?
3. Do you think about money?
4. What do you think about when you think about money?
5. How do you feel about money?
6. When you spend money, how does it make you feel?
7. Which are you with regard to money: a thinker or a feeler?
8. Have you ever made a major purchase based only on emotion?
9. How did that purchase work out?
10. What would you have done differently?
11. Does this give you a little insight into how you think and feel about money? Let's now examine your money belief system.

CHAPTER THREE

IT'S ALL ABOUT YOU AND YOUR MONEY BELIEFS

BACK AT THE MALL

It's Sunday afternoon, the day after the big concert. You had a good time, but the performance didn't seem to live up to all the hype. You mumble to yourself, "My Dad would go nuts if he knew how much I spent last night. Let's see: ticket $75.00, parking $25.00, snacks $38.00, t-shirt $50.00, CD $25.00, and another $45.00 for a late dinner. Wow, that adds up! I can't believe I spent so much. I wonder if I can take the camera back I bought at The Mall yesterday. That will save me some money. I didn't even use it." You look at the receipts and realize that you put everything on the credit card you just transferred the balance from. "This is going to be a problem. I guess I need to put that card away. But I can't do that. I need it for emergencies." You chuckle, lock your card away in your desk, and think, "Yeah, like the limited-edition tour t-shirt—priceless." Mall 3, You 0.5 (half a point for locking up your card).

You pack up the camera and head off to The Mall. You think to yourself, "I don't get it. I try to do the right thing with my money, but it never seems to work out very well. I can't believe I used that credit card last night. Mom and Dad are so good with money. And my sister always seems to have her act together. I wonder why I'm the way I am and they are the way they are with money." As you turn into the mall you tell yourself, "Just return the camera and don't spend any money!" You park as close to the camera store as possible and start to say out loud, "I only have cash, and The Department Store isn't going to get me this time."

You enter the side entrance of The Mall and head directly to the camera store. You notice that all the fall fashions are out—nice. "Not this time. I can't afford it. Last year's clothes will have to do." You feel good about yourself. You return the camera for a credit and start back to your car. On the way out you pass a book store. You notice a display of new books and see that there are two or three books on money and personal finance. "I think I need to see if any of these books can help me. I need to change something, or I'll be broke." You go in and begin to browse the offerings. "They all say the same thing, or they're just a rehash of stuff I know but just can't seem to do." You find one that looks interesting. "Maybe this one is different. I guess I'll find out." You turn to go to the checkout and you overhear a sales clerk recommending a book on how to change behavior and make better choices to a customer. You think, "I wonder if that's what I need—a behavior adjustment. Maybe my problem with money is all in my head, and not learning a new way to budget."

You pick up the book and read the title, Better Choices: When We Know Better We Do Better, by Dr. Faye Hargrove, PhD. "Hmm, this is different. It says that we are all products of our past experiences. We can't change the past but we can learn from it. Cool, no more $50.00 t-shirts or credit-card roulette." You skim the table of contents for key concepts and terms: "Prisoners of Our Perspectives, Learning to Let Go, Releasing Stored Fear and Guilt, Peace of Mind, Limiting Belief, Breaking Bad Habits, and other good stuff. This is all about *me. I bet it will help, or at least be a good start." You put the first book back and buy Faye's book—with cash. Mall 3, You 1.5.*

WHAT HAPPENED AT THE MALL?

Do you get it yet? Money is not about stuff, it's about behavior—your money behavior. In the story, the concert cost you a lot more than the cost of a ticket. Not considering your time, your spent $183.00 on extra stuff and paid for it with a credit card you should have cut up right after you transferred the balance. The spending made sense to your feeling brain at the time but didn't seem like such a good idea to your thinking brain the next morning. However, you were able to rationalize all the spending. What happened? Simple; you had a spending event just like the one at The Mall when you bought the THING. Your feeling brain trumped your thinking brain. In fact, based on the situation you put yourself into, you were destined to spend. You were overpowered by a cascade of "feel good" brain chemicals and a money belief system that said, "It's okay to open the wallet!"

You did recover a bit the next day when you and your thinking brain made an inventory of all the stuff you bought—good thing your thinking brain can add. Your thinking brain was not very impressed with the cost of the concert and went to work to try to make everything better. It came up with a plan. You should return the camera and put away your credit card. It even helped you overcome your guilt and regret about your spending—your brain can be your friend.

By now it should be obvious that your feeling brain is ready and able to take advantage of any and all spending opportunities. And if you let it, your feeling brain will spend all your money, whether you are at The Mall, a concert, or anywhere else you happen to be. You are spring-loaded to spend. All you need are the right conditions and presto, you are the proud owner of something new and shiny. It doesn't matter if you "need" the stuff. Your feeling brain doesn't care as long as it makes you feel good. Then, after you spend the money, your thinking brain kicks in to beat you up with a dose of buyer's remorse. If you're lucky, your thinking brain then mercifully rationalizes the entire experience and you eventually feel better about your money behavior. Trust me, there are better ways to run your budget.

Did you pick up on the fact that Dad would not approve of your spending? How about that your parents and sister seem to manage their money behavior better than you? What's that all about? Maybe something happened in your past that continues to influence your spending behavior today? You also had some significant "Now-I-Get-It" moments. That's good. Your thinking brain kicked in and got you thinking long term and about being accountable for your money behavior. You even took proactive steps to control your spending—like putting away the credit card, paying cash at the book store, and avoiding a spending situation (when you parked near a side entrance to The Mall, it made it a little more difficult to spend). Most importantly, you started to examine your money behavior with the intent to understand, and maybe even change it. Fantastic. Understanding your spending behavior is more complicated than just blaming every purchase on your biology and out-of-control feeling brain. You can do this occasionally for the magazine purchase at the checkout, but I think you need something more to explain the $800 custom-made Kevlar and Corinthian leather golf bag—although, the titanium rivets were a nice touch. Right? Note: Yes, you'll look good at the first tee, but the bag will do nothing to improve your game.

YOUR MONEY BELIEFS

Can you see now why money makes us all so crazy? Just about everything we do costs money. And it's next to impossible to escape the "spend more and feel better" message that has crept into every facet of modern life. This message is pumped into our heads 24/7 in ways we couldn't have imagined just a few years ago. Our feeling brain loves it. Our thinking brain hates it. Our pocket books can't support it. And our money anxiety goes through the roof. Help . . .!

Dr. Faye (yep, the author of the book you bought at the book store; she's a strategic partner of our firm and we use her research and tools with our clients) tells me all the time, "Ted, how you behave today is simply a reflection of all your past experiences and feelings. And you see the world through your own filter based on those unique experiences and feelings." Wow! Smart lady—that's why we like to work with her. When I buy something stupid (I'm usually okay with my purchase; it's my wife or someone at the office who points out that I made a feeling brain money choice— we are the pros at this, you know) Faye will pull me aside and say something like, "Ted, you have a money belief system that works off your values, temperament, and past feelings. If you don't like the way you spend money, you can change. You just have to let go of your past money mistakes and negative feelings about them, reframe, and move on." Piece of cake...

Let me give you an example. I think I'm the only guy in my profession who doesn't play golf. I'm a triathlete—although old and slow. My daughter got me started a few years back after being a runner all my life. I love the sport. At my age (currently 59) I'm about as fast as I'm going to get. The odds are, I'll get slower but not much faster. Here's my problem. My feeling brain does not accept this. My feeling brain tells me that I'm 25 and still able to run a three-hour marathon—not going to happen. My feeling brain tells me I can roll back time and get better. All I have to do is buy more stuff and train harder. And I know this is true because I read *Triathlete* magazine, I participate in Ironman events, and I belong to a Tri club. My feeling brain sees me in the pictures going fast. At the events I feel the excitement of participating, and the Club reinforces all the above.

If you don't know much about the sport, it's not really complicated. You swim, then ride a bike, and then run—although, sometimes over ridiculous distances. You may have done this as a kid every day, all summer long, growing up. And it didn't cost much. Fast forward to today. The sport can get expensive. It's no longer cut-off jeans at the lake. Now it's paying for pool time, special wet suit, and maybe a coach (I thought I could swim until I tried my first open-water event). Bikes have become an art form. You can spend more on a top-of-the-line bike than I did for my first new car. And running shoes can cost a lot more than my first pair of Keds—a lot more. My feeling brain loves all this. My thinking brain rationalizes all this. If I'm not careful, I can spend a small fortune trying to squeeze out a few seconds of speed.

Right now I have a bad case of bike envy. All the cool kids have new bikes. Their bikes have all the cool go-fast stuff. They look fast standing still. Their wheels cost more than my bike. I don't feel as confident when I'm with them. I don't think they'll want to play with me unless I look just like them. If I only had a better bike, I'd go faster. If I go faster, I'll do better in races. If I do better in races, people will treat me differently. I need a new bike. So if I work hard and save my allowance, maybe my mom (wife, husband...) will take me to the bike store to get one.

I'm a financial advisor. Better yet, I'm a behavioral financial advisor. I know exactly what is going on in my head. My thinking brain is working overtime to beat down my bike envy. My belief system—my values and temperament about money—is working overtime to come up with some kind of compromise. My past experiences and feelings about a bike tell me I need a new bike.

The Triathlon culture says I need a new bike. My truly rational thinking brain—and my wife—think I'm nuts. Why would anyone my age and ability spend thousands of dollars on a bike? That kind of money could be used for so many important things—retirement, bills, expanding the business, or something my wife wants. But people who are judging me about a bike don't see or feel the same way I do about a bike. Their feelings and frame of reference about a bike are different than mine. They see a bike through their filter. So, who's right? It depends on your perspective. The truth is, how you frame the money problem will give you the "correct" answer. The challenge is taking the time to understand the issues and objectively reframe. I'm crazy for wanting a new bike and everyone who disagrees with me is also crazy because they don't understand why I need a new bike. I do *need* a bike. They think I just *want* a new bike. MONEY MAKES US CRAZY...

Where are you in this discussion? What kind of "bike" do you need? Why do you need it? What beliefs are in play that influence your point of view? Taking the time to know and understand your money beliefs will go a long way toward helping you achieve money sanity. There is significant research on this topic. And, as you'd expect, there are differing opinions on how and why we spend the way we do. In fact, the relatively new field of behavioral economics has evolved from traditional economics to study and address these questions. Much of this research is way beyond the scope of this book. I get excited about all this; but you might not, and I need you to stay awake long enough to finish the chapter.

Money sanity implies a healthy relationship with money. I believe a healthy relationship with money simply means that you "get it." It means that you realize that money is simply a tool—a means to an end, if you will. Money is the common denominator of modern life. You can't live without it, but sometimes it is difficult to live with it. When handled well, money will give you peace of mind in your chosen life style. Think of money as the grease that helps make your life work. For that reason, it's important to know about your money beliefs.

Dr. Faye, who is an Industrial Psychologist and President of Hargrove Leadership Services, has spent years helping people make better choices. She does this by helping them identify and modify their beliefs about any number of behavioral issues—to include money. Faye has given me permission to go over some of the key points of her book. If you want to learn more about Faye and her book, check out www.betterchoicebook.com.

I'll try to paraphrase her extensive body of work on belief systems and changing behavior. This is all good stuff. It works, and our clients love it.

- You cannot change the past.
- You can learn from the past.
- You can make peace with the past and accept it.
- You are able to change how you feel about past events.
- You can let go of your feelings about a past event and release its power over you.

Your past choices and experiences define how you feel about money—now. If you grew up in a home with a healthy outlook on money, there is a good chance that you now have a more positive money belief system. If, on the other hand, you had bad money experiences somewhere in your past, then your money belief system will likely be negative. But here's the kicker. If you don't like your current money belief system, you can change it.

So what are limiting money beliefs? They are any beliefs about money that make it difficult for you to make good money choices or cause you to have negative feelings about your money choices. For example, let's say that when you were growing up you were taught that it was "bad" to spend money on "nice things from a place like

The Mall." Now, as an adult, you feel guilty and experience buyer's remorse when you shop at The Mall. In order to overcome your limiting beliefs about money, you must first identify them and let them go. Once you really let go of your limiting beliefs, you can start to develop a healthy relationship with money.

Let's go back to my bike dilemma to work through what Faye is saying. As a kid I lived on my bike. I loved it. It gave me mobility, freedom, and speed. I can remember vividly my first bike—when the training wheels were removed and when I moved up to a "three-speed racing" bike. These feelings are etched into my brain. I also know it was a stretch for my dad to buy bikes for me and my four brothers and sisters. When I got the "three speed" I was expected to "take care" of it—the money doesn't grow on trees discussion followed. This event helped shape my values about money and buying and owning things. These values are now part of me. I also know that delayed gratification is not one of my strong suits and that I like nice things. I am fully able to rationalize a quick purchase of something I think is of high quality and that I "need" now. I can also trace this behavior back to earlier money experiences. Part of my belief system is that spending money can make me feel good, that nice things are better than "settle for" things. I know I should work and save before I buy "nice" things, but I'd rather not. I also know that nice things on sale are better than nice things at full price. Therefore, I'm a sucker for a sale. As a result of my occasional lack of money restraint, I've at times bought stuff I did not really need with money I did not have to make me feel good. And I'd rationalize it as a good buy because it was on sale and I really saved a lot of money. Whether or not the purchase made sense in the grand scheme of things was not important. As you'd expect, some of these purchases caused some anxiety and regret—or at least some heavy second guessing. For example, when I bought my first Tri bike I thought I had taken the time to buy it right. It was a pretty red one that was on sale (I did that part right). But looking back, I should have taken more time to really examine what my expectations of the bike were. If I had spent a little more money I could have bought a better bike that would have lasted longer—at least that's the way I see it.

I've learned that I can change my money beliefs and money behavior if I simply learn from my past "mistakes." First I have to stop beating myself up about the bike purchase. Based on the information I had at the time and my skills at the time, the bike I bought was more than adequate and in fact served me very well for a number of seasons. I learned that I'd drive myself nuts if I always have to have the best. Today, best means "best for me, given the situation." I now look at that bike purchase very fondly and I really think I made a good money decision. When I buy a new bike—yes, I will because I have to—I will reframe my bike buying event in terms of what I learned during my last purchase. I'll also try to objectively view the buying event through my new filter based on my modified money behavior.

Later in the book you'll learn how to use the *Money Behavior System* to make better money choices. This is the system we developed to help people like you and me make better money choices. The system helped me align my spending with my values, temperament, and knowledge in a way that works for how I think and feel about money. The story about my bike envy is a snapshot about my relationship with money. What the story doesn't show you are the steps I've taken to make sure that the truly important things about money in my life—taking care of my family, being a good steward of my money, and so forth—are taken care of before I ever consider buying a new bike. My feeling brain likes to dream, but my thinking brain is in control. Remember, you can feel good about money, eliminate all of your limiting behaviors, and still make some pretty dumb money choices. Spending a few thousand bucks on a new bike if I have a large credit card balance is just crazy. And as much as my feeling brain wants the bike, my thinking brain is not going to let that happen.

What's your favorite money story? Was it a bike, car, investment, vacation, or something else? Admit it; you are just like me and a few million other people when it comes to money. Here is a key point about your money belief system. It's your belief system. As long as you are not clinically dysfunctional with your money—we aren't going there in this book—you are okay. Be careful not to judge yourself and others too critically. The term "healthy money belief" is very subjective. I'm talking about fine-tuning your money behavior so you can sleep at night, not doing a complete behavioral makeover. Reframing your "I wish I could do over" money choices is simply looking at the event in an objective and positive light. You don't get a do over—what's done is done. What can you learn from the event? Accept what you did, make peace with the decision, and move on—it is what it is. Make the event, as uncomfortable as it might be to you, a positive learning experience and don't let the event negatively define your relationship with money. You can change your money beliefs.

Keep in mind, your money behavior has nothing to do with the amount of money you or your family had. There are many people with a very healthy attitude toward money who grew up in modest or poor households. There are also many people who were surrounded by wealth growing up who are dysfunctional with money. This is about your money *behavior*. It is not about your money. Remember, your money beliefs drive your money behavior. And you learned your money beliefs somewhere in your past.

KEY POINTS

- Realize that your perception of money influences or filters all your current money choices.

- Understand that you can change or reframe your perception of money by letting go of negative money feelings and your limiting beliefs about money.

ACTION STEPS

Ask yourself, or better yet, write down your answer to each of the following questions:

1. You learned to think and behave the way you do about money from your childhood. When were you first aware of money? Was this a positive or negative experience? Why? How did the event make you feel about money? Do you still have those feelings about money?

2. Your beliefs about money can be empowering and resourceful or limiting and hinder you from reaching your financial goals. What do you believe about money? Do you think money is positive or negative? Why? Describe a situation when money was empowering and resourceful. Why did this make you feel good? Describe a situation when money was limiting or hindered you from doing something. Why did this make you feel bad?

3. Your values, beliefs, and money temperament drive your money behavior. What is important about money to you? What do you believe about money? How does money make you think and feel?

4. Conflict can exist in a relationship if individuals do not share the same or complementary belief systems about money. Is there someone close to you who has a different money belief system than you? What is different? How do these differences affect your relationship?

5. You can assess and recognize whether or not your approach to money is empowering or limiting. Review your last 10

to 20 major money transactions. Were these positive or negative experiences? Why?

6. Limiting belief systems can be reframed. You can let go of unhealthy attitudes about money and learn new behaviors. Do you have a negative belief about money? Why? Can you restate this belief in a positive way? Can you find a way to turn your negative into a positive?

7. Reframing your limiting beliefs and letting them go does not necessarily guarantee better money decisions. You may still spend money on crazy things; you'll just feel better about yourself afterwards. Assuming you have identified and let go of one or more of your limiting beliefs, do you think you now have a healthier relationship with money? Are your money choices more aligned with what is important in life to you? When you make a major money decision do you now stop and think or do you simply act?

Congratulations! You have just fine-tuned your money belief system. Now, let's head back to The Mall to find out how the rules of money have changed.

CHAPTER 4

THE RULES HAVE CHANGED

THE MALL—AGAIN

I t's been at least nine months since you've been back to The Mall. In that time, you've paid down your two credit cards and built up a cash fund. You text your friends that you are about to leave the house and that you will meet them at the newly renovated "North End of The Mall." A co-worker was there yesterday and said it was fantastic—all new design, lots of technology, and new stores and restaurants. You grab your keys and put the grand-opening discount flyer in your pocket. Mall 4, You 5.5 (Mall point for getting you back into The Mall).

You feel great about tonight. You've just received a promotion to VP and a nice bonus. You make a quick voice note to yourself on your smart phone, "Call HR: review benefits and change 401k." You think to yourself, "I really need to get my money act together. I've wasted a lot of time." You navigate to your bank account to confirm that your bonus has posted. "Super! This is going to be a good night. I can update my wardrobe for the new job, check out the new gear at the electronics store—a 3D television is the next big thing—and maybe a cruise." You chuckle and confirm to yourself, "I deserve this. I've worked hard." You make a mental note:"Don't forget to save enough to open that Roth IRA that dad keeps nagging me about." You run to your car. "Life is good. Things are so different than they were when I was a kid."

The renovated Mall is fantastic—everything is state-of-the-art technology, plus new colors, new smells, and new sounds. A "Mall Guide" meets you at the door and explains all the new features of The Mall. The Guide also helps you download a new application for your smart phone. The app is cool. It automatically notifies you about Mall discounts and promotions and offers buying suggestions based on your spending behavior. And for only $9.99 a month, you get a "Personal Buying Service."A Mall Guide will make gift suggestions and even shop for you. You think, "Cool! I think this will help me in my new job." You sign up and say to the Guide, "Is this a great country, or what?"

You move on to meet your friends at a trendy new restaurant near The Mall entrance. While you are waiting for your order, someone you assume to be a server stops by and thanks you for dining with them. You ask, "You look familiar. Where do I know you from?" The person smiles and says, "We went to high school together. I was a good friend of your sister. I've been away for years and just returned to town." "Oh, yeah, I remember," you respond in a matter-of-fact way. "Jenny Miller! It's great to see you again. I think the last time we talked was just before I left for school and you were working at a restaurant downtown." Jenny gets a coy smile on her face and says, "I'm still serving food." You nod in a slightly patronizing demeanor and smile. She adds, "Yep, this is my eleventh place. Things are going well. I got into this right after culinary school at City Tech—best two-year investment of my life." The blood drains out of your face and she quips, "I have to go, the mayor just arrived—appetizers are on me. By the way, your sister says things are going well for you, too—we tweet. Congratulations." Wow! You're impressed. Jenny Miller owns all this! You immediately text your sister...

"I have to admit, the meal was great. Let's get going. We have a lot of ground to cover and not much time." You pick up the tab (you're the one with the money), leave your business card for Jenny with a short thank-you note, and you and your friends head into The Mall—ready to spend. You don't disappoint. In three short hours you update your wardrobe, buy a flat-panel 48-inch LCD television (the 3D technology isn't quite there yet), and book a cruise. With your last discount coupon and your last dollar, you stop by the book store and buy a few books on investing. You say to your friends, "I guess it's time to figure out how to make some real money."

On the way home, a small voice rises up inside your thinking brain and says, "Nice job, big shot. You're out of control with your money. This isn't your grandfather's economy anymore. Enjoy for now, but your money behavior has to change." Mall 10, You 5.5.

WHAT HAPPENED AT THE MALL?

You were ambushed, bushwhacked, mugged, and beaten up by your animal instincts and your feeling brain. And you didn't feel a thing. You seemed to have left your thinking brain in your car while you were in The Mall. Too bad it didn't "wake-up" until you were driving home—it could have saved you a fortune.

Do you see a pattern? You—your money beliefs and behavior—are both the cause and the cure for your money affliction. You were off to such a good start. You had not been to The Mall for months. Super job—you paid off your credit cards and built a cash reserve. Your career seems to be on track, and you were just promoted. You have even earned a nice bonus—I guess "had" is a better word. You seem to have lots of nice stuff. By contemporary standards and common wisdom, you are doing everything right and should be on top of the world. You work hard, and you do deserve to reward yourself from time to time. Your new position and station in life seem to dictate a particular lifestyle. You are confident in the future and in your ability to control your destiny. Of course everything will be okay. You've rationalized your behavior, and you have books and other resources that support your assumptions. Your mentor and the good folks on HGTV (cable lifestyle shows) have the lifestyle you want. So you spend money the way they do in order to have the things they have—it's human nature and the American way. But think about this: what if the money culture you are so comfortable with, the culture that supports and even enables your spending behavior, is wrong? What would you do? What should you do? Can you adapt? What if you have no choice? Well, the rules of money have changed. The old ways of spending money and managing money don't work as well as they used to. Just look around your city, your neighborhood, your office, and your home. Do you know people who were doing everything "right" and still lost their jobs or had their benefits cut back? Do you know anyone who was in a "safe" investment who lost a lot of money? Do you know any recent college graduates who can't find a job? The rules of money are different than they were just a few years ago. And as my friend Tony Jeary likes to say, "Things are changing at the speed of life." Are you ready?

THE RULES HAVE CHANGED

"Are you ready?" That's a tough question. The future is coming at you faster than ever before. As soon as you think you know the rules about money, they change. What worked yesterday might not work today. What works today might not work tomorrow. Confused, overwhelmed, anxious? You should be. I'd be concerned if you weren't. Don't feel like you're the Lone Ranger on this one. Almost everyone I know feels the same way. And you wonder why money makes you crazy? This might be why:

- You are bombarded with more money choices than you can possibly process. Too much choice is not always a good thing.
- The new economy is very different than the economy of your parents and grandparents. What worked for them might not work for you.
- The financial services industry is in transition. In many cases, the industry is reinventing itself on the fly. Expect new products and services, new regulations, and new technology.
- Today, everyone is self-employed. You may not think of yourself as self-employed, but you are. And you need to start acting like you are running a business.
- In the end, you are accountable and responsible for your money outcomes. You have to get it right—the consequences of failure can be harsh.

More choice is not always a good thing when it comes to your money sanity. Your brain doesn't like ambiguity; and if there are too many choices, it shuts down. You think you want lots of choices. You think it will make you happier. But in reality, all the options just make you crazy. Consider the simple act of buying a pair of jeans. Once upon a time it was easy. At the start of the school year, moms across the country went to Sears, Ward's, Grant's, Penney's, and the like and bought their children a couple of pairs of jeans for school. They probably didn't care much about brand or style. And they might not have even cared too much about fit—I've seen the pictures. If the jeans made it through the school year, they were either "passed down" or cut off for shorts. Nothing complicated about any of this.

Buying jeans will never be that easy again. Even though you can buy jeans just about anywhere (good), there are thousands of possible jean choices (bad). As my daughter informed me, you don't just walk into a store and grab the first pair of jeans you see—even though they may be the brand and style you've worn for years. You have to take your time and consider: brand, cut, color, style, quality, price, size, use, fashion, culture, peer influence, and a number of critical features and benefits known to only a select number of jean connoisseurs. I never knew this, but the jeans offered at one store might not be the "same" jeans offered by the same manufacturer at another store. The difference is so slight that only a teenager can tell the difference—usually just before you are leaving the house to go somewhere important. Buying jeans is now hard work and big business.

In the grand scheme of things, the consequences of not having the perfect pair of jeans are small (my daughters strongly disagree with me on this one). If you make a mistake and buy a "bad" pair of jeans, it doesn't take much effort or money to fix the perceived error. Better yet, just reframe and wear them—at least in the yard. This is not the case with your large and significant money choices—house, car, investments, retirement plan, insurance, college, and so on. You seldom get a "do over" if you choose poorly. If you do, the cost in time and money is usually huge. As you'll learn later in the book, your money values, temperament, and knowledge are significant factors in how you make money decisions. The point is, too many choices and too much information, under the right conditions, will make your head "explode." And this is perfectly normal. Don't believe me? Instead of jeans, let's consider something as basic as barbecue sauce. Head down to your local "150,000-square-foot we-sell-every-kind-of-food-possible" supermarket and try to pick out a bottle. There are hundreds of choices. Now consider something really important with real consequences. Break out the mutual fund offerings for your 401k and try to pick the "right" mix of funds from the list. See what I mean? Money makes us crazy. By the way, which did you put more time into—sauce or funds?

The rules of money used to be fairly simple: study hard, get a good education, get a good job, and retire in a nice place with a good pension. If the college route was not for you, you could always get a good-paying job at the local plant making something and still end up with a good pension. It was not unusual for people—families—to spend their entire lives living and working within just a few miles of where they were born. It was not unusual for someone to spend his or her entire career with one company. Not anymore.

Things are different now. You are now defined by what you know and do, and not by who you work for. Traditional education is still important, but so is life-long learning. The skills and knowledge you have today might not be relevant tomorrow. The traditional four-year college diploma you are so proud of might not be as valuable as a technical certificate or technical degree. I have clients with technical degrees who are doing significantly better financially than some of my liberal arts grads. Traditional manufacturing jobs are being replaced by knowledge-based jobs. And because of technology, knowledge-based jobs can exist anywhere. All you need is the internet, and you have an office.

Just because you're really good at something does not mean you'll always have a job. The best you can hope for in today's economy is the opportunity to work. Unfortunately, this does not guarantee your job. Life is not fair. Job security today is more a function of the status of the contract you currently have, the quality of the last presentation you gave, the behavior of the last client you saw, and the state of the technology you currently use. Information, knowledge, and technology are the real game changers. This is the new economy.

Unless you are in complete denial, you know things have changed. You also know that things will continue to change—fast. The question, then, is what do you do to cope with the change? Good question. First, to be successful in the future—peace of mind in your chosen lifestyle—you must reframe who you are and what you do. Today, everyone is self-employed. You really are. You exchange your skills, knowledge, and abilities for money in the marketplace. Don't confuse what you do with how you get paid. There are lots of legal structures that get you paid—employee, consultant, contractor, or business owner. The point is, you own the means of production—you. So, Boss, here is what has to happen: regardless of what it is you do to earn money, or how you get paid, you are in charge of you. And as a business owner, you are responsible for three key things: generating income, supporting your lifestyle, and creating real wealth. That's it. Everything else is details.

Here are a couple of things you need to know about your business. First, your business is a system. Systems are designed to accomplish something. And all systems have four basic components: input, process, output, and feedback. Second, what is the name of your business? I have a very simple name for my business; it's "Ted McLyman." A better name might have been, "Ted's Grand Adventure Tours," but I digress. The key point is that I'm in the business of me. You, on the other hand, are in the business of you. Here's your basic business structure.

> (Name of Your Business)
>
> *CEO:*
> You
>
> *Board of Directors:*
> Anyone who gives you advice or counsel necessary to run your business profitably.
>
> *Input:*
> Anything and everything you do to generate real (after-tax, inflation-adjusted) income.
>
> *Process:*
> Your lifestyle—your stuff and what you do to generate true wealth.
>
> *True Wealth*
> What's left over after your lifestyle that increases in value or generates additional real income.
>
> *Feedback*
> How are you doing? What needs to change? Who will make the change?

And you thought you needed an MBA to run your business. You don't. All you need is a little common sense, some discipline, and a plan like the one I will introduce in the next chapter. Like I said earlier, managing money isn't rocket science—but you do have to get on the rocket.

As in every business, money is critical to your success. You have to find a way to make money (cash flow), and you to have find a way to keep as much of it as possible. Your business needs to have a profit (this is not a dirty word). You need to have more money coming in than is going out (these might be a dirty words to some). Your ultimate goal is to run your business so that when you stop working, you can maintain your chosen lifestyle. Listen closely: there are only a couple of ways you can do this. You either have to find a job with a pension that will provide this income (adjusted for inflation) or you have to do all, or a part of it, yourself. And the sooner you decide which you want to do, the easier it is.

Where do you find a job like that? Off the top of my head, I can't think of any. If there are some, they are a well kept secret. That means it's up to you. To live the lifestyle you want in the future, you have to build your wealth now (wealth is not a dirty word, either). If at the end of you working career your net worth (assets minus liabilities) is negative or too small to do the things that are important to you, you'll have a serious problem. Deciding which color vest you want to wear at the local big-box store because you don't have enough income is not how most people want to live their later years. Your challenge is to make a money decision as soon as possible to live with freedom and dignity in the future. Unfortunately, your feeling brain doesn't like to plan very much. Your feeling brain likes the shiny new car much more than spending the money on a retirement plan.

Think about it; is this any way to run a business? I don't think so. Do you know any successful business owners whose goal it is to work in their business for 30 or 40 years, only to sell it for so little money that they have to go back to work? I don't. Then why do so many people with jobs think they can spend all their money while they are working and expect to have enough when they retire? They don't get it. And remember, life happens along the way—that also costs money.

Think about this: Bill Gates is giving away his wealth, not his lifestyle. Wealth (at whatever level) gives you options, leverage, and flexibility. If you want to control the shots, you need to be in control. Whether you like it or not, that requires money.

Run your life like you are running a business. You have to make a payroll every month. You have to pay the bills. You have to market and promote yourself. You have to offer the best "you" possible to your market. You have to invest in your business. Your business has to be profitable.

As a business owner and a person who helps businesses be profitable, I suggest the following:

1. Successful business owners know what business they are in and are honest about their capabilities and limitations. What do you enjoy doing? What are you good at? What are you passionate about? How can you turn this into a career?

2. Good business owners, when they can afford it, outsource or delegate everything they aren't very good at, don't have the time to do, or that takes them away from their core business. Do you do your own surgery? Never! Then, unless there is some compelling reason to do otherwise, why do you do your own taxes, sell your own home, or act as your own financial advisor? These are full-time professional careers. Why do you think you know something they don't know? What gives you the edge they don't have? The money pros get it wrong; what makes you think you can do a better job, considering your current knowledge, resources, and available time? Build your board of directors and key advisors. Then use them.

3. Good business owners know the rules and adapt when necessary. The rules about money you grew up with probably don't work as well today as they did for your parents—if they even worked for them. Money rules are always changing. It's your responsibility to keep up with the changes and adapt.

Telling everyone you "didn't get the memo" just doesn't cut it. When was the last time you did a complete review of your business and your business plan?

4. Good business owners invest in themselves first. Successful business owners know that it's all about cash flow and capital reserves. What do your income statement and balance sheet look like? If you had to sell your business today, what would it be worth? Would anyone want to buy it? How are you investing to maintain and improve your business?

5. Good business owners are growing. Are you?

ACTION STEPS

Consider the following actions and questions, and write down your answer to each:

You are the boss—take charge:

1. Benchmark where you are financially.
2. Inventory your skills, knowledge, and ability.
3. Are you in the right career? Do you like what you are doing? Are you good at it?
4. Do you have a passion for what you are doing?
5. Does the career you're passionate about support your lifestyle? If not, what needs to change—your lifestyle or your career?
6. What things are you doing (time- and money-wise) that take you away from getting the most out of your career? Are these things important? If not, what happens if you stop doing them? If they are important, what happens if you delegate them to someone else? Most importantly, do you also have balance in your life?
7. Tony Jeary, in his book *Strategic Acceleration,* says that creating superior results faster requires clarity, focus, and

execution. Do you have clarity, focus, and execution for your life's plan?

It's good to be the boss. And every successful business is built on and guided by some basic values. Let's next examine what is important about money to you and clarify your money values.

PART II

MONEY BEHAVIOR SYSTEM

So far, we've established that:

- Money makes us crazy and sometimes stupid.
- As humans, we are not naturally wired to do well with money.
- All money decisions are emotional.
- Our belief system influences how we think and feel about money.
- You can fine-tune, even change, your money belief system.
- Modern life is complex and fast moving, with too much information and too many choices.
- The rules of money have changed.
- Today everyone is essentially self-employed and needs to manage his or her money like a business.

Early in the book I asked you to observe how and why people make money choices. Have you formed an opinion or fashioned a point about people and money? What did you learn? Do you think people as a whole are rational spenders? Maybe you know some people you think are "crazy" because of the way they spend money. Keep in mind, you are judging through your eyes and not theirs. They might think you're the crazy one because you don't spend the way they do.

If everyone were rational all the time, Facebook and YouTube wouldn't be any fun. Suppose you got a tattoo sometime in your past. You proudly posted a picture of it on Facebook. Everyone loves it—well, almost everyone; you forgot that your mom has an account. When you got the "tat," was it a feeling-brain or thinking-brain moment? Did you stop to consider that you might have to explain why you have a tattoo to your grandchildren someday? I doubt it.

And when the grandkids ask, and they will, what are you going to tell them? You could say, "Everyone thinks and feels differently about how to best spend their disposable dollars." On the other hand, the academic approach might be better: "The marginal utility was greater than the marginal cost. Therefore, the expenditure was a rational use of my scarce resources." No one talks that way. Maybe you could discuss the differences between the primitive feeling brain and the modern thinking brain. Nope, how about the truth? "I made an important money decision in a place named The Drunken Sailor Bar and Tattoo Emporium. And now I have to live with it."

As you know by now, money decisions are complex and emotional. Some decisions have minor consequences. Others can be catastrophic—or hopefully, just embarrassing. The trick, as I've said before, is to keep the big money mistakes to a minimum. Cashing in your retirement plan to buy a timeshare is not a good decision. Adding Moose Tracks ice cream to your shopping cart is okay—in moderation.

If you really want to make better money decisions, and I assume you do, you need a system to help you control your feeling brain and engage your thinking brain. Believe it or not, many folks are able to do this. What separates them from the "spending challenged" is how they approach their spending choices. Financially successful people have a deliberate strategic system to help them make better money choices. People with money issues tend to use an impulsive and emotional approach. This approach usually doesn't work.

Therefore, if you are serious about managing your money behavior, you need a system. However, your system must fit you—how you think and feel about money. A "one-size-fits-all" approach might not work.

You'll find your solution in Part II. It's called the *Behavior Money System*. It works for our clients, and it will work for you.

CHAPTER 5

MONEY VALUES

YOUR MONEY VALUES

You plop yourself down on your new leather couch in front of your new LCD television and start to mindlessly channel surf. You say out loud, "Wow! This has been a great month." You sit back and reflect on what has happened during the month. "We had a great cruise. Everyone had a super time. That was a trip for the record books." You stop on a channel, look briefly, and move on. "The new job is going to work out just fine. I did well! Nice raise, lots of new responsibility, and my own office—with a decorating budget, to boot. Who would have thought...?" You continue to surf, "Dad and Mom are visiting next month. They're going to love the new office. I'm glad I'm meeting with the office design folks tomorrow morning." You finally find a channel that catches your attention—at least for a few seconds: "Sherpas of Tibet. Aren't they the guys that haul all the gear up the mountain and give advice to mountain climbers? That's what I need, a Sherpa—someone to follow me around and give me advice and keep me out of trouble, especially with my money." For some reason, thinking about your dad's visit has forced you to consider all the money you've spent the last couple of months. "Dad will love the television, but there is no way I'm going to tell him that I spent my entire bonus on all this stuff."

You pick up a pad of paper and start to doodle. You draw a mountain and a stick figure. You continue to play around with the figure while mindlessly listening to the television. After a few attempts, you end up drawing a faceless stick figure that looks like it's hitting itself in the back of the head with its hand. You look at the figure and smile. "That's what I need every now and then—a whack on the side of the head to keep me focused and on course with my money. I sure could have used a good smack at The Mall last month. I can't believe I spent the entire bonus!" You look at your paper and put your pencil at the top of the mountain and think, "Apex. That's the top of the mountain. I think I have a name for my Sherpa." And you print "A. PEXX" next to the stick figure. You smile and think, "A. Pexx, I'm keeping you on my shoulder. When I screw up and want to spend money on something stupid, you can smack me on the side of the head." Your phone rings and you answer the call. It's the office design team; they'll be at your office tomorrow morning to start the design process.

Back at home the next night, you sit down to go through your mail. You open your statement from The Mall for your "Personal Buying Service," and before you can say anything a small voice in the back of your head says, "This is your guide, A. Pexx. The Mall got you on this one—$120 bucks for nothing." You shudder a little and immediately realize you bought a one-year contract for something you'll never use. You think you hear a soft snicker in your ear.

You immediately think there has to be a better way to manage your money. "If this keeps up, I'll be bankrupt." And a voice says, "Sit down and go through the values drill, just like the office design team did with you this morning. But look at your money values instead of your office values." Hey, why not? The team took you through an *exercise to help them figure out what was important about an office to you. They ended up with a nice list of values—the things you find most important in an office. You were impressed with the team. They were different than what you'd expected. They didn't have any product catalogues or samples of stuff—just a note pad and a few forms. You remember saying, "Cool! They aren't sales guys like the last group."*

So you sit down with a piece of paper and start through the process they used to identify your office values, hoping this will help you identify your money values. You remember terms like Neuro-Linguistic Programming, Strategic Acceleration, and values propositions, but you don't remember exactly what any of that meant. You do know that you enjoyed the process; and at the end you had clarity, focus, and a positive action plan. You thought, "Let's give it a try—nothing to lose. If this can help me save some money, I'm all for it."

You pull a copy of the "Office Value Worksheet" from you briefcase and study it. You cross out "office" and replace it with "money." You look at the modified form and think, "I bet this will work fine with money." A. Pexx chimes in: "I know it will." Mall 10, You 7.

WHAT HAPPENED *AFTER* THE MALL?

For the last four chapters, you've been watching a "shadow" of yourself having a grand time spending money. The money behaviors described in the stories are a reflection of your "values." Values are the things that are most important to you in life. They act as a filter to your behavior. They help you sort information and put it into general categories. According to Dr. Faye, your core values were formed and established by the time you were ten years old and reside in your subconscious. Your values motivate you and provide a benchmark to evaluate your behavior and the behavior of others. You have values for everything from your personal relationships to the kind of car you like to drive. You have money values. And your money values are the foundation of your spending behavior. The *Money Behavior System* was designed to help you make better money choices by understanding your behavior. The System begins with identifying what is important about money to you—your money values.

Your money values are the most important things in your life that cost money or take money to accomplish. You have "Big V Values" and "little v values." Your Big V Values are your core values, the critical things in your life. These are the things that get you up in the morning. They get you motivated to act. They may involve sacrifice. They can be your basic needs—food, shelter and safety. They can also be your more complex higher order needs—social acceptance or self-esteem. Your key money values, if not supported, accomplished, or satisfied, cause you great emotional or physical pain.

Your Big V Values are big and important and generally not "things." These might include: career, relationships, family, health, fitness, personal growth, spirituality—you name it. It doesn't matter what the values are, as long as they are important to you and cost money. Your higher order values are your most important "ideals," regardless of what other people think about what you are doing with your money. Check out the booster and legacy gift list from your school for some interesting Big V Values. What do you think about the people who leave millions of dollars to their pets in their wills? Do you share the same values? They think it's important, and it's their money.

Small v values are not as lofty and often are associated with tangible things or goals. They might include: new car, new home, education, retirement home, and hobbies and activities—like golf, skiing, sewing, painting, running, and so on. Your feeling brain loves a lot of the small v values.

You have your own set of money values. They are both important and unique to you. No one should judge your values—assuming they fall within accepted social norms. If your legacy is to have the restroom at your college's freshman dorm named after you, so be it. You just need the money to do it. You might also have to explain it to your spouse.

Let's walk through the values exercise that got all this started. At the end of the exercise, you should have a nice list of your Big V and little v values. Let's begin:

1. Find a quiet place and take out a piece of paper or notebook.

2. Quickly list the things you value in your life. Just make a list. There is no right or wrong response.

3. Quickly list the things you want to accomplish or achieve in your life.

4. Quickly list the things you want to own or acquire in your life.

5. Quickly list what you want people to say about you and how you want to live your life.

6. Write down how you'd live your life if money were not a problem.

7. Go over your lists and identify the items that take money to support or accomplish. Put a $ next to each item.

8. Next to each $ put your estimate of what it will cost today to accomplish it.

9. Now, go over all your lists and put a big V next to your big V values and a small v next to your small v values.

10. Finally, number your top five big V values and your top five small v values.

You have just created your money values profile: the five big things and the five little things that are most important to you. These form your money values. Look at your list.

- How important is money to you?
- Do you have the money to do everything you most value?
- How does that make you feel?
- Does that make you think about money differently?

If this is confusing, or if it's difficult to get started, try this: take out your bank statement (electronic or paper) and your calendar. Look for patterns in what you do, where you spend your money, and what you spend your money on. This can be interesting. I have clients who tell me that their highest value is a comfortable retirement. But when we go over their checkbook and calendar, we discover that their time and money are going someplace very different—to golf, cars, jewelry, horses, and other "now" stuff. Their money behavior is different than their money values. Something has to give. It's okay to have a value of golf. It is also okay to have a value of a comfortable retirement. The question is, do you have the money to do both? If you don't have enough money, what are your options? What are your priorities? Do you need to change your "business" plan? You'll have to make a money choice—there are no do over's.

Everyone should identify his or her money values. It's that important. It may also surprise you to learn that your spouse's or partner's money values are different than yours. It may also be sobering to learn that your money values and behavior are out of sync with the people around you. If you are the only one in your office who is into collecting vintage wine, you may feel a little lost. On the other hand, if everyone has the same money values (depending on the value) you could have some interesting "group think" about money. I've seen a lot of strange spending behavior just because everyone in a car pool was a golfer, hunter, collector – you name it.

Tony Jeary takes a different approach with his clients. He has them, and their spouses or partners, mark their top ten core values from a pre-prepared list of core values. He then has them rank the top 10 values by priority. Give it a try. His list is provided below.

- Financial security
- Respect from others (those who know you)
- Recognition—to be well known to other people
- Personal freedom and independence
- Family structure and cohesiveness
- Spirituality and faith
- Organized and clean structure of environment
- Organized structure of personal routine and schedule
- Punctuality for self
- Efficient use of time
- The want of personal solitude
- Power over others
- Personal creativity
- Accumulating knowledge
- To be appreciated
- To be enjoyed
- To take on challenges
- To experience excitement and adventure
- To compete
- To be productive
- To feel inner peace
- To experience love and affection
- To be of service to others
- To interact with others
- To gain wisdom and insight

- To enjoy cultural activities
- To have intimate (truly honest and close) relationships with others
- To be creative
- Lifestyle

It doesn't matter which technique you use, as long as you take the time to clarify your money values. This does not take that long, and it will give you great insight into your spending behavior.

Very few people—including money pros—take the time to identify their money values. They go right into goal planning. Here's the problem with that: traditional goal setting doesn't go deep enough. Core money values bring up deep emotions. They are what make you tick. Goals usually are neither as deep nor as emotional. See if this helps:

I value good health and fitness. It is part of who I am. I have been health conscious and fit ever since my mom dropped me off at the YMCA for swimming lessons. I also like the personal challenge of endurance sports and the lifestyle that goes with it. So here is how a money-values discussion about fitness may go with me:

- **"What is important about money and fitness to you?"**
  "It allows me to compete in triathlons."
- **What is important about triathlons to you?"**
  "I like the personal challenge and the state of high fitness they require."
- **"What is important about the personal challenge and state of high fitness to you?"**
  "It allows me to achieve my physical potential."
- **"Is there anything more important than achieving your physical potential to you?**
  "No."

In this short (and shallow) example of money values, my Big V Value is to achieve my physical potential. It is not to compete in a triathlon or buy all the Tri gear. Many people and money pros never get past the small v value of a goal (new bike). A goal discussion might go like this:

- **"Is there anything you'd like to buy or have in the next two years?"**
  "Yes, I'd like a new bike."
- **"In today's dollars, how much does the bike cost?"**
  "About $5,000."
- **"If I can show you a way to get the bike in the next two years is there any reason we can't get started today?"**
  "I guess not."
- **"How much money do you have to work with?**
  "$1,000 cash, and I can put away $100 a month."
- **"Great, let's get started."**

Do you see the difference? This is not to say that goal setting is not important. It is, and we will spend time setting goals later in the system. What I am telling you is that you have to take the time to clarify your money values before you do anything else. Knowing what is important about money to you is critical to giving you money sanity. Your money values are the glue that holds the *Money Behavior System* together.

You need to take the time to work through your money values to the point that you know what is truly important to you. These are your highest order money values. These are what get you out of bed in the morning. These are what make you sacrifice, and these are what make you "you." Don't forget, it can be the brass plaque over the restroom as much as it can be to go on a mission and save the world. It's your money value.

KEY POINTS

- Values are the things that are most important to you in life.
- Values filter the information you receive about the world around you.
- Values determine how you spend your time and money.
- Values apply to everything from cars to relationships.
- Values are established early in life.
- Values can change over time.
- Most people do not know their money values.
- Most money professionals focus on goals, not values.
- Know your money values to promote your money sanity.

ACTION STEPS

Ask yourself, or better yet, write down your answer to each of the following questions:

1. What is important about money to you?
2. What motivates you?
3. What are your top five Big V Values?
4. What are your top five little v values?
5. Is your spending behavior aligned with your money values?
6. Is your current financial plan built on money goals or money values?
7. What are the consequences of failing to achieve your highest order money value?
8. Have you taken steps to make sure this does not happen?
9. What must happen to insure you accomplish your highest order money values?

You have now laid the foundation of the *Money Behavior System*. Next, we'll head back to The Mall and identify your Money Temperament.

CHAPTER 6

MONEY TEMPERAMENT

YOUR MONEY TEMPERAMENT

I t's the next day, and you are sitting at your desk reviewing your notes from the office design team and reviewing their proposal. "Wow! These folks nailed it. They captured everything I find important in my office. They are awesome. Only the best for me! I do like the good life. Good thing it's not my money—but I would have spent the money anyway. You only go around once." A. Pexx cynically mutters, "Yeah, that's because you're a spender."

You gaze down at your desk and see the notes and lists you made last night trying to figure out your highest money values. You look at the picture you sketched of A. Pexx and sigh, "A. Pexx, old buddy, I wish it were as easy to identify my money values as it was to design my office. I've never thought about my money values before. And my money is important. You'd think I could find a book or someone who could help me with my money. Maybe I'll give Dad a call when I get home. He's always been so levelheaded with his money. I bet he's still got the first dollar he ever made." A faint voice in your head speaks up and says, "You're not at all like your dad. He'd drive all over town to save a penny on a pack of gum."

You look at the plans again and grin. At the same time, the President sticks his head in your office and says, "Let's get lunch at Jenny Miller's new place at The Mall. I'll introduce you to Jenny if she's there—my treat." You quickly explain that you and Jenny are good friends and think to yourself, "Miller knows the President! Who would have guessed?" You grab your jacket thinking, "Good thing I bought the designer label."

You and the President drive up to the valet parking entrance at The Mall. You feel pretty special. When you get out of the car you think, "This land yacht cost more than my parent's house." The President sees the expression on your face and says, "It's used. I never spend good money on things that lose value." "Hmmm, I never would have guessed." SMACK! "Listen up! That one went right over your head."

You are relieved to learn that Jenny is out of town, visiting one of her other places. You are escorted to your table and sit down. You carefully follow the President's lead when you order, and A. Pexx whispers, "Don't mess this up." You pass the "what- to-order-at-lunch test," and the President begins to tell you how happy everyone is with your work and that they have big plans for you. You flush a bit. The President then looks you in the eye and asks, "Who's your money person? The reason I ask is that the person you replaced lived a bit extravagantly for my tastes." How do you answer a question like that? You think, "I expect the President to have money people. But for me? I've never thought about it." You give a knee-jerk response, "I do everything myself. I'm pretty good at it." And a faint voice asks, "How's that working out for you?" The President smiles and leans forward. "I thought so. Let me ask you a question? Did you decorate your own office?" The President stands and hands you a business card and says, "Give these guys a call. They're like office decorators for your wallet. They helped me a few years ago with my money. I think you'll like them." Let's go. We have a meeting to get ready for." Mall 10, You 8. (A. Pexx gives you a "layup" for not buying anything.)

All day long you keep thinking about what the President said. "What does decorating my office have to do with my money? The company is paying for all this. I just show up, tell them what I think and feel, and they do all the work. I'll give these money guys a call right after I call my dad." You drop the business card in your desk drawer and reach for your cell phone to call your dad. A. Pexx stands and mumbles, "You'd better not lose that card."

Your dad is a retired civil servant who worked over 35 years at the same job. He now lives in a nice golf community. Before you call, you think, "Dad and Mom have it pretty good—social security, nice pension, and full medical benefits. I think he's making more now than when he worked. They are able to do more now than we ever could when I was a kid. I guess things are different now." You dial the number and your mom answers. After some small talk, she says, "Your dad is driving me nuts. He's obsessed with his money. He joined a new foursome, and now all he talks about is money. His new friends were big-shot business owners, and they've convinced your dad that he needs to be more aggressive with his money. They all have these "trader" accounts and special software. They said that it's so easy to do on the computer." You think, "Dad doesn't even like computers. And the most aggressive thing he's ever owned is a money market at the credit union." Mom adds, "Now he just sits in front of the television and yells at the guy on the business channel!" A. Pexx sighs. "Interesting learning point..."

Your dad gets on the phone, and the first thing out of his mouth is, "I've been trading small caps and I think I'm doing okay." You respond with surprise, "Dad, small caps—what are you talking about?" Your dad excitedly says, "Yeah, I'm getting some good tips from my golf buddies on how to make money in the market. I've taken some of *my retirement money and started buying stocks online. It's easy. Just look 'em up and push a button. It's just as easy to sell. Oh, it's good to hear your voice. We're excited about seeing you next week, but talk fast. I have a trade in, and I have to see if I got it. You know how much I hate to lose money. By the way, you need to start watching the money shows on cable. They'll open your eyes. I've been doing this all wrong for years." You catch your breath, and a voice says, "Big trouble! Back away from the phone—now." Your dad gives the phone back to your mom so he can check his trade, and you tell her that you need to talk when they visit. And you think, "I can't believe Dad is day trading. He doesn't have the temperament for it. What he's doing would drive me crazy." SMACK! "Don't you get it yet? Money choices are all about your unique money temperament—how <u>you</u> think and feel about money."*

WHAT HAPPENED?

Just like the story about your first trip to The Mall, there is a lot of thinking/feeling brain stimulation going on here. You are excited about your new office. Lunch with the President was great, but had you questioning your money values. The President seems to think and feel differently about money than you. The design team is very cool because they captured the way you think and feel about your office. And your dad has reframed his money values and you think he is spinning out of control—because you know his money temperament can't handle the risk.

Here's the potential problem: you and your mom perceive your dad as risk-adverse and conservative with money. His new money behavior worries you because it seems so out of character from what you expect. You and your mom "see" your dad as a conservative saver. His current behavior surprises you because his "new" money values seem to be out of sync with his money temperament. It appears Dad's golf buddies have shifted his money values. It remains to be seen if his money temperament supports his new values. And all of this is driving your mother crazy.

Welcome to the world of money temperament. Your money temperament is simply how you think and feel about money—either rational or irrational. It is, in my opinion, the most important part of the *Money Behavior System*. Knowing this is critical to your money success. Your money temperament may or may not be aligned with your money values. This can be a problem for you. Remember when you wanted both the new car and the comfortable retirement? You chose the new car. That's a temperament issue. Money temperament is about behavior and filters and perception. Your money temperament is a very human part of your money behavior profile.

Money temperament is the critical piece that is missing from most popular money guides, and it is seldom mentioned by people in the financial services industry. In fact, traditional economics does not even acknowledge that behavior matters in economic choices. (It appears that economists don't go to The Mall much.) However, you know that how you think and feel about money does matter. Temperament is all about how you frame your money decisions and ultimately make your money choices. Unfortunately, your temperament doesn't always get it right. The trick is to be aware of your unique money temperament, gather all relevant data, and try to make the best money choice you can. If it were easy, you'd never make a "bad" money decision. Can you find the faulty reasoning in these examples?

- You buy a stock on a tip from a friend who has made a great deal of money in the stock market. The stock drops in price and you sell at a loss—you blame your friend for the loss. Or, the price goes up and you sell for a profit— you're a genius.

- You have a large balance in your no-interest checking account, and at the same time, you have a large balance on your high-interest credit card. Your highest return is to pay off your credit card. You don't do this because you don't want to spend the "vacation fund."

Behavioral economics is all about addressing issues like these and trying to figure out why people make irrational money choices. The research and literature on this subject are complex, technical, and evolving. However, for our purposes, you can develop a good understanding of your basic money temperament by answering three simple questions:

- Do you like to spend your money?
- Do you demand the "best" in every money decision?
- Do you like to take risks with your money?

SPENDER OR SAVER?

Off the top of your head, do you think you are a saver or a spender? On a scale of one to ten, with one being a saver and ten being a spender, how would you rate yourself? I've found that when I ask clients this question, they are very accurate with their perception of themselves. Answer these questions:

- Do you have an emergency cash account?
- Do you generally pay with cash/debit card?
- Do you have a budget?
- Do you fully participate in your retirement plan at work?
- Do you have investments and savings outside your retirement plans?
- Do you use shopping lists or preplan your purchases?
- Do you avoid making major purchases when you are emotionally down?
- Do you research your major purchases?

- Do you discuss your major purchases with someone before you commit yourself to the purchase?
- Do you balance your checkbook and reconcile your credit card statements?

The more "Yes" answers, the more you tend to be a saver. The more "No" answers, you can't pass-up a sale.

Assuming you have a healthy relationship with money, I don't care if you are a spender or a saver (I bet you never thought you'd hear that from a money guy). However, I do care very much that your spending supports your money values. If you tell me one of your critical money values is financial freedom, then I assume you will spend money to make it happen. And this is *not* buying a lottery ticket once a week. This is what makes me crazy about money.

Instead of trying to change your spending behavior—which is difficult—I'd rather build a money strategy around your temperament. In other words, it emotionally "hurts" when you try to change your basic spending temperament—so why try when you have so many other important things to do with your life? Again, assuming you aren't out of control, doesn't it make more sense to just accept your spending behavior and build behavioral nudges, incentives, and controls that complement and support your temperament? That's how successful diets and exercise programs work. For example, I have a client who just can't seem to save money. He says he has a savings account, but he's never seen an ATM he doesn't like. His savings account is really a cash account that he keeps in a machine. To help get his arms around his spending temperament, I made it easy for him to save and difficult for him to spend. I opened a savings account for him that was very inconvenient for him to get to. The bank was out of town and had no ATM or electronic privileges. If he needed money from his savings account, he had to do everything by U.S. mail. I could have set it up in an account that requires two signatures, or in an account that requires a large minimum balance with high fees if the balance drops below a certain amount. The point is, the solution focused on the desired outcome—savings—and not on the behavior. You could say that we reframed his relationship with his money—and it worked.

What happens if you are a spender who is in a relationship with a saver? Is there potential for issues? A strong saver with a strong spender might be an explosive combination. If they are closer together in temperament, the issues might not be as great—maybe even balance each other out. One of the biggest challenges I face is a strong spender in a relationship with a strong spender—tough to plan. However, two strong savers in a relationship have their own unique issues. Sometimes it's tough to convince two people who have been saving all their lives that it's okay to spend their money—even the principal. Hey, just another way to drive you crazy—with money.

MAXIMIZER OR SUFFICER?

Maximizers are the folks who always want the "best" in their money choices. Now, there is nothing wrong with wanting the best value from your money choices. You work hard for your money. No one is going to begrudge you that. However, some people take this to the extreme. If you've ever been in sales, you will recognize this temperament. These are the clients and customers who are never satisfied. These people have very exacting expectations about service, quality, value, and performance. If their expectations are not met, they can't emotionally handle it. For example, let's assume you are a maximizer and own a mutual fund. Suppose the fund doesn't perform to your expectations (up or down). This will bother you emotionally and may cause you to act irrationally—sell the fund for the wrong reasons or even blame your advisor. (As much as we try, we can't predict or control the market.) At the extreme, maximizers are difficult to work with and very unhappy. Sufficers, on the other hand, are just the opposite. Think of them as the 85-percent- (or whatever number less than perfection works for them) solution folks. They find the emotional and real cost of trying to get the other 15 percent too high. They have more realistic expectations, are easier to work with, and are generally happier with their money choices.

Below is a survey we use in the office to help our clients figure out if they are maximizers or sufficers. Complete the exercise. I think it will give you a new insight into your money temperament.

Instructions: Circle the number by the answer that *best* **reflects how** *you* **feel about the stated situation.**

A. When *you* are shopping for a car:
   1. I hate shopping for a car; I'll go to the dealership that has a car I've liked before and just buy one.
   2. I don't mind checking out a couple of dealerships to see what might fit my needs at a decent price.
   3. I prefer checking out several dealerships so I can get a good balance of price and what I'm looking for in the car; I may even visit some dealerships twice to be sure.
   4. I want the best deal; I'll even work up a spreadsheet with features and prices to help me decide.

B. When *you* are shopping for canned soup:
   1. I'll always go for the store brand, provided I've tried it and it's okay.
   2. If the price is decent or there's a sale, I'll buy a national brand of the one I want.
   3. I always go for the premium label, because I need some assurance I'm getting the best.

4. I check out the price per ounce on the shelf, balance that with the brand's reputation and my experience, and then I can make a cost-benefit decision on which to buy.

C. When *you* are writing a friend:
1. I usually just get a hi-how-ya-doing card, stamp it, and get it in the mail.
2. I will occasionally get a blank card and write a couple of lines.
3. I often take the time to write out a page of stuff on my computer and then enclose it in a funny card.
4. I wouldn't dream of anything but a three- or four-page handwritten note on nice stationery.

D. Having regrets on *your* everyday decisions:
1. I generally don't feel it's worthwhile to revisit decisions—I always make the best one I can with the information I had available at the time.
2. I usually don't have regrets, unless something just happens to pop up shortly after I made the decision that throws a whole new light on the issue.
3. I tend to be careful in my decision making, seeking out information and recommendations; but in the end, it's my call.
4. I like to write down the pros and cons of a decision, maybe rank them or score them on importance, and often think about it overnight before taking action.

E. *Your* view on collaborative decision making:
1. I generally don't need to wait for another opinion. I just go ahead with my best info, insight, and instinct.

2. I usually consult with a trusted friend with expertise or with my spouse before I make all but the most routine decisions.
3. I often want to get other opinions or additional information before making a decision so I can have some assurance that my decision is a good one.
4. I like to set a deadline for a decision and find out everything I can up to that date, so I can be sure that my research is thorough and complete.

Scoring: Total the numbers you circled. Lower score is more sufficing; higher score is more maximizing.[1]

Is your temperament what you expected? How about your spouse or partner? Is this one of the reasons money makes you crazy? My high maximizer clients can be difficult to work with. What I do is make sure all expectations are expressed before a money strategy is implemented. These people have to know what may or may not happen with their money, what to expect, and who is responsible for what. They also have to know exactly what they can and cannot control—like the market. Sometimes nothing I do is enough. In these cases, I either do not take the person on as a client or I fire them. Yes, advisors can "fire" their difficult clients. We also deserve money sanity.

RISK TAKER OR RISK AVOIDER?

What is your risk profile? Are you risk-adverse, risk-neutral or a risk seeker? Do you have the same risk tolerance in every situation or with every product and service? Does your risk profile change when you are under stress? Do you have the same risk profile as the people around you?

---

1   Maximizing/Sufficing assessment instrument extracted with permission from the Apexx Money Temperament Profile Questionnaire, Copyright ©2010, Apexx Behavioral Solutions Group, LLC.

Everyone has his or her own risk profile. Men appear to seek more risk than women. Your risk profile is situational. It changes over time and according to the things going on in your life. If you naturally tend to be risk-averse, you will only take on added risk if you get something in return to offset the risk (pain of loss).

Risk is contextual and personal. You need to constantly evaluate your money in terms of your life situation and risk profile. You are busy. You have things going on in your life. Don't forget to keep your money aligned with your risk profile. Don't allow yourself to go into retirement with the portfolio of a 25-year-old.

- Do you know where your money is?
- Do you know the relative risk of your investments and saving accounts?
- Do you know the risks of all your money products and services?
- Do you know what kind of insurance (all kinds) you own?
- Do you know if you have the right kind of insurance?
- Do you need to update or modify your insurance?
- Do you do things with money that scare or frustrate your spouse, partner, children, lawyer, CPA, banker, or financial advisor?
- Do you consider yourself risk-averse, risk-neutral or a risk taker? Why?

YOUR TEMPERAMENT IS BIASED

Okay, you have a new snapshot of your money temperament. Do you think it is accurate? Here is another issue you need to be aware of: your money temperament might be biased. It might cause you to make money decisions based on bad or incomplete information. It might cause irrational choices. Again, money does make us crazy.

You have perception issues. Words sway you. You have money biases—in your thinking about money, not socially. Think of a bias as a rule-of-thumb. It provides you a general framework to make a decision, but it might not be very accurate. For example, suppose everyone you know seems to be investing in a local bank stock. You buy the stock because, "Everyone can't be wrong." They can, and you could lose your investment.

Humans tend to use faulty reasoning, poor logic, and bad information when they make decisions. Behavioral economists and psychologists have identified hundreds of biases. They absolutely influence your money choices. When you make a money decision based on a bias, you do not have all the facts and can miss information that is critical to your decision making. Here are some examples of a few key biases:

- Endowment: "My house is worth more than the market price." If you own it, it is worth more.
- Loss Aversion: "The market is dropping like a rock. I'm selling." Losing money hurts more emotionally than making money.
- Overconfidence: "I'm a successful doctor. I know I can run a restaurant." Just because you are good at one thing, it does not mean you are good at something else.
- Confirmation: "I know I am right. Look at all the stuff I found on the internet that supports my decision." You look for information that confirms your decision.
- Self-Attribution: "I'm a great stock picker. My portfolio is up ten percent." Your successes are because of your ability, but your losses are not your fault.
- Illusion of Control: "I attended a seminar on options trading and bought their software. Now I can beat the market." You can't control or predict the future—really, you can't.

You use biases, or rules-of-thumb, because they make life easier. Think of them as "lazy" decision-making tools. You could not live without them. However, you need to engage your thinking brain every time you have to make an important money decision.

KEY POINTS

- Your money temperament is how you think and feel about money.
- Your money temperament is unique to you.
- Your money temperament influences your money choices.
- Your money temperament is biased and sometimes leads to bad money decisions.
- You need to know your money temperament to make better money choices.
- Your money temperament should align with your money values.
- Your money temperament drives your money strategy.

ACTION STEPS

Ask yourself, or better yet, write down your answer to each of the following questions:

1. Are you a spender or a saver?
2. Are you a maximizer or a sufficer?
3. Are you a risk taker or risk-adverse?
4. How does your money temperament influence your money choices?
5. Who do you know with a different money temperament than you?
6. What makes you crazy about their spending?
7. How do you make them crazy with your spending?
8. Do you think you make rational money choices? Why?

Armed with your new understanding of your money values and money temperament, let's next talk about how you gather and process information about money—your money knowledge.

CHAPTER 7

YOUR MONEY KNOWLEDGE

WHAT YOU CAN LEARN AT THE MALL

*Y*ou get back to your office late in the day after a long meeting with a maximizer customer. You lean back in your chair and moan, "Perfectionists drive me nuts! I can't believe it took a vice president, a district manager, and our attorney to come up with something this guy could live with. They don't pay me enough for this." A. Pexx chimes in, "Yes they do—that's why you have a custom office." You look at the clock and remember that you have to stop by Jenny's restaurant and make a showing at a party for an associate who was "outsourced." You think, "It doesn't seem fair. I wonder if it could happen to me. SMACK!" A. Pexx nods in the affirmative and says, "You really don't have any savings. What would you do?"

You open your desk drawer to retrieve your keys, and you see the card the President gave you at lunch. You put the business card in your pocket and think, "I guess I'll give these guys a call." You grab your coat and start to head for your car. "Why not call them now? I guess if they're good enough for the Boss, they should be good enough for me." You call and leave a message for someone to call you in the morning. When you turn to lock your door, it hits you, "I get it! I didn't design my own office. I worked with a professional. Why wouldn't I do the same thing with my money?" A. Pexx nods, smiles broadly, and lets out a loud whistle of approval. As you pull the door shut, you think you hear something. You look down the hall and see nothing, shrug, and head to your car—A. Pexx gives out a loud "Outstanding!"

As you walk to your car, you run through the key points of your customer meeting. "I can't believe that guy. We gave him our best presentation, and he didn't seem to understand a word I said. I wonder why? He seemed like a bright guy. I'll call a meeting tomorrow and have the sales manager check the numbers and add a couple of spreadsheets to fill in the holes." You recall reading something about how people learn and process information on Dr. Faye's web site. You make a mental note to yourself to log into the site and check it out.

You park near the front entrance to The Mall and head directly to Jenny's. You feel almost like you have blinders on, and A. Pexx leans over and whispers, "You're off to a good start. Keep moving."

Jenny's is packed, as usual. You work your way through the crowd to the room reserved for the party. You enter the room expecting a "funeral" and find a celebration instead. Everyone is congratulating Juan and his wife. Your body language screams, "I don't understand?" The person standing next to you gives you an understanding nod and says, "It must be nice to be able to open a new business on the same day you lose your job." You nod and move closer to Juan. You think, "He looks great—not a worry in the world. What gives?" You walk over to Juan and congratulate him. "Too bad about your job, but I guess everything is working out for you." Juan smiles, "I saw this coming a few years back. It didn't make any sense to keep the Division here. So I saw this as an opportunity to finally do something that I've always wanted to do. I'm just so lucky that the President hooked me up with Tonya Reeves. She helped me do all this. Thanks for stopping by." Before you can respond, someone grabs Juan and starts talking with him. A. Pexx leans in and says, "Look at the card." For some reason, you take the business card out of your pocket again and look at it. "I thought I recognized the name."

As you start to leave after the party, you start brewing again about your difficult customer. "Why didn't he get it?" Then out of nowhere it happens. The Mall and all of its sensory power engulf you. You feel good. On the way to the bookstore, you pass a leather goods store. In the window is the most beautiful leather case you've ever seen. You stop and look at it. Then you move to the doorway and pop your head in. The smell of expensive leather is intoxicating. You hear cool jazz playing softly in the background and you enter the store and move directly to the display of briefcases. You pick out a deep black-colored bag with a satin finish. It feels wonderful—smooth, soft, and expensive. When you open the case, the smell of "quality and wealth" overpowers your senses, and your feeling brain screams, "I have to have this." An impeccably dressed sales assistant walks over to you and says in a confident, sophisticated voice, "You have an eye for quality leather goods. What do you expect of a product like this?" A. Pexx starts beating the back of your head and screaming, "This is not the bookstore." You answer, "Exceptional craftsmanship." And the sales assistance asks, "May I ask, what is important about exceptional craftsmanship to you?" A. Pexx, in a panic, screams, "You can't afford it. You have higher priorities. You don't need another briefcase." You notice that there is no price tag, only a code—a good indicator that the bag will cost more than your mortgage payment for the month. WHACK! WHACK! A. Pexx hits the alarm, and your thinking brain finally kicks in. You smile, return the bag to the display, thank the sales assistant and confidently leave the store. A. Pexx smiles and states,

"Glad you got your act together. I thought I might have to call the Marines to rescue you." Mall 10, You 10.

Back in the car, you feel good about yourself. You look at Tonya's card again and think, "I'm looking forward to this call. I need to get home and do some research." A. Pexx applauds.

WHAT YOU LEARNED TODAY

Just another day at work, having to deal with thinking and feeling brain issues—yours and everyone else's. Your maximizer customer seems to process information differently than you. He has his set of filters and you have yours. The economy is still changing; and as Juan demonstrated, people can adapt if they are prepared. It appears that successful people have coaches—especially money coaches. Looking good and having stuff is not a long-range financial plan. It also appears that solutions that are tied to your values and temperament have better outcomes. Finally, The Mall is designed to engage all of your senses and the power of your feeling brain to make you spend money. Your thinking brain can keep your feeling brain in check, but it is a difficult, full-time job. Knowing what you want in the future and why it is important to you will help you stay the course. We'll cover this more in Chapters 8 and 9. Before we go there, let's focus on how you take in and process information.

WHY MONEY KNOWLEDGE?

Step three in the Money Behavior System is your money knowledge. In step one you identified your money values—what's important about money to you. In step two you identified your money temperament—how you think and feel about money and the things that are important to you. Step three is money knowledge. This is both what you know about money and how you process money information.

Here is the challenge of the day: not only are you not wired to work well with money, but you most likely don't have the technical skills either. Don't take this personally. It's not your fault. Our society doesn't spend a lot of time training people about money and personal finance. And if you are fortunate enough to have taken a class at one time, I bet most of the skills and knowledge are no longer relevant. I'm in the industry, and I know how difficult it is for me to keep up with everything—laws, taxes, products, services, technology, markets, and more. As good as you think you are with money, you can't know it all because you can't physically keep up with all the information (and still have a life). Everything about money has gotten too complex and sophisticated. And technology has compounded the problem. Contrary to what you read and hear, predicting the future still is not an exact science. Computers are wonderful for looking into the past, to spot trends that don't exist in order to make bad decisions worse. Maybe I'm just a cynic. Don't get me wrong, I own lots of computers. I've just been around long enough to know what financial garbage looks like; even when it's wrapped in a pretty folder carried by a smart person in a suit. You need basic financial literacy skills—then delegate the hard stuff.

The money industry is immense. It produces huge amounts of information daily. Twenty-four hours a day money people collect, analyze, and distribute trillions of bits of information. Reporters, researchers, analysts, experts, pundits, politicians, academics, advisors, planners, sales representatives, your brother-in-law, the girls at work, and your college roommate are all part of this. Unfortunately, your brain can't process all this stuff. It's like buying jeans—too much information. To make things worse, a lot of the information is outdated, inappropriate, biased or just wrong for you. So, what should you do?

- Understand that information is not knowledge. You only have money knowledge after information is received, processed, put in some kind of category, and stored for future recall. The problem is getting your brain to move it from information to knowledge. Sometimes you receive good information but reject it. Your brain does this because either you don't know it's good information or you don't think you'll need the information. For example, if you are not in the market to buy a car, you probably don't spend much time looking at car ads. This is "good" information but not very helpful. You will tend to flush this information and move on to more important stuff—anything you are interested in.

- Realize that the majority of the money industry focuses on products and services, not values and temperament. Therefore the information it provides is mostly about features and benefits—supported with piles of historical data, graphs, and charts. Your challenge is to find the products and services that are best suited to your values and temperament. This is not as easy as it sounds. Common wisdom suggests that all you have to do is buy a list and pick. Not so fast. How was the list put together? Who put it together, and why? How do you know the current number one is a good fit for you? How do you know if you have the right list? Be careful with lists.

- Know that the financial industry thrives on numbers. We have numbers and statistics on everything. Unfortunately, most people aren't very good with numbers. To really have money knowledge, you have to know the numbers. Too many numbers makes your brain hurt. Given enough time and data, the industry can prove just about anything. When you get a product kit, check the numbers to make sure you understand what they mean. Most people fall in love with the pretty pictures and never question the numbers.

- Know what you do not know. You have neither the time nor the capacity to know and do everything related to your money. Teams of pros with PhDs manage money 60 to 80 hours a week, and they get it wrong. As a part-timer, do you really think you can beat the pros? If you like this stuff, then find your niche and master it. Lots of people lost a great deal of money in real estate during the last recession, simply because the cable shows made it appear so easy to make money.

- Finally, conduct a money knowledge inventory. Do you know how you process information? How do you handle stress? Down markets hurt more emotionally than up markets make you feel good. If you don't understand a money choice or don't have the temperament for it—don't do it!

YOUR MONEY FILTERS

Learning how you process information is critical to your money sanity. Dr. Hargrove has graciously let me share her adult learning style inventory with you. This is the same process we use in the office.

I'm going to summarize (almost copy—thanks Faye!) and explain her ODEE Style Inventory™ below. You can find the complete ODEE Style Inventory™ in the appendix or online at: www.hargroveleadership.com. I recommend you take the inventory after you read this chapter.

Dr. Faye developed the inventory to help her clients better understand how they process and communicate information. I use it with my clients to help me determine how they process and filter money information. We are both interested in essentially the same thing—how your brain filters all the information it is subjected to every day. In the simplest of terms, you use your senses to filter information. Once the information is filtered, it is stored and can later be recalled. Most people have one primary and one secondary filtering system to take in information and communicate what happened. This inventory will help you determine the style or system you use most of the time. And sometimes you change styles, depending on the situation and context.

Here's the psychology stuff...

- There are four filtering styles
  - Visual (see—eagle)
  - Auditory (hear—dolphin)
  - Kinesthetic (feel—elephant)
  - Auditory Digital (procedures—owl)

- Visual (see) people tend to learn or memorize things by "seeing" pictures. They rely mostly on their sense of sight to take in and process information. If they can't "see" it, they may not understand or remember the information. Visuals like written information, notes, diagrams, and pictures. They memorize by seeing pictures in their minds. If they don't write information down, they tend to lose it. Visual people are very good at working with colors and pictures and using the "mind's eye." They are usually neat and organized and good note-takers. When a visual communicates, they use words like: see, look, view, appear, show, dawn, reveal, envision, clear, foggy, and so on. They talk like this:
  - Do you see what I'm saying?
  - If I could show you…

- Will you look at my proposal…?
- If this looks good…

- Auditory (hear) people tend to learn or memorize best through sounds and the spoken word. They understand new ideas and concepts best when they hear the information. They are easily distracted by noise. Auditory people sometimes have a remarkable ability to repeat back what you tell them, word for word. They learn best when they can concentrate on the words and tone of voice of the speaker. They will tend to listen to a speaker and then take notes afterwards. Often information written down will have little meaning until it has been heard. When an auditory communicates, they use words like: hear, listen, sound(s), in tune, be all ears, and so on. They talk like this:
  - I can't hear myself think!
  - Do you hear what I'm saying?
  - If I tell you...
  - If this sounds...

- Kinesthetic (feel) people tend to learn through feelings, touch, movement and space. They learn skills by imitation and practice. They are intuitive. Before accepting an idea, a kinesthetic must *get a feel* for what they are doing. They use body language to communicate and may touch people when they talk to them. They can typically do more than one thing at a time and may get bored **if required to sit for long periods of time.** They would rather play sports or do a craft than sit still and read a book. They tend to be physically active and enjoy the outdoors. A kinesthetic uses words like: feel, touch, grasp, get hold of, get my arms around, solid, concrete and so on. They talk like this:

- I can't put my finger on it.
- My gut tells me something isn't quite right.
- I could help you get hold of…
- If this feels good to you…

- Auditory digital (process) people want order and want to make sense of their world. Attention to detail and wanting to know exactly why things are the way they are is one common characteristic. They like information. They memorize by steps, procedures and sequences. They look for rational explanations, think logically, and seek logical answers, facts, and data. When making decisions, auditory digitals are more likely to accept an idea or proposal when something has been measured, categorized, analyzed, or quantified in some way. They use words like: sense, experience, think, learn, process, know, perceive, and so on. They talk like this:
  - Does it make sense?
  - How long will it take and how much will it cost?
  - I can help you know…
  - If this makes sense…

Did you find your style? Can you put a friend's name with each style? Is there a style you have difficulty working with? About me: I'm a Kinesthetic (feel—elephant) and very verbal. I think out loud—fast—and I like wild ideas and new challenges. I can drive an Auditory Digital (procedures—owl) nuts. I can do detail work and a dueling spreadsheet, but I prefer public speaking, marketing, and business development. I was very successful as an agent/registered representative (sales guy, back then) but naturally gravitated to management. I'm a big-picture, delegate, and get-out-of-the-way guy. Sometimes after I get all excited about a new project that I thought up (and in my mind is already completed and I'm moving on to my next idea...), I have to stop and look back to make sure there is anyone behind me as I charge forward. I need to balance my style and the way my brain works, so one of my partners is a retired Navy Captain, a nuclear engineer, and a math major. His job, besides being our CFO, is to keep me from leading everyone off a cliff. I'm the visionary optimist and he's the realist. It works well for us.

Here's a style problem I've observed within the finance industry—we have a lot of owls. And I mean big, aggressive "number-crunching" owls. This species likes to flock together. Owls are good people and they mean well; unfortunately, many of the people who need money help the most aren't owls. They don't think like owls and they don't talk like owls. Many owls don't understand this. They continually force their non-owl clients to suffer through mountains of data. The owls love this stuff. But everyone else sees, hears, or feels something else. By the way, this is why the presentation with the customer went so badly. The owl lawyer sucked the life out of the poor guy (definitely not an owl), one spreadsheet at a time. There are times when it is important to know and match styles.

True story: A few years ago I attended a meeting in Boston hosted by a large mutual fund company. Most of us who attended from the field were not owls. For those who don't know, Boston is an owl sanctuary, so every presenter was a super owl. The last speakers one afternoon were two PhD owls with loads of degrees in quantum number crunching (one was French and the other German). I could not pronounce the subject of the presentation (it was in English), but I do remember words like "probability," "risk," and "this time is different." It was the kind of presentation that begins like this: "I know these screenshots are busy and difficult to read but..." and doesn't stop until slide 32 or 57—I can't remember. They argued in a foreign language (I assumed it was German) for what seemed like an eternity. They stopped when I agreed to stop banging my head against my table. Here's a solution. If your money pro is great with your money but not great in matching styles and presentation, try this. Tell him or her what you expect. Share your style. No one ever does this. You're the client; we work for you, so it's all about you. We're the ones who should adapt, not you. If you aren't into money details and numbers, that's okay. Demand the executive summary. Money is too important not to communicate well.

Last point—The Mall. Malls and other spending retreats are traps. They are designed to stimulate all your senses. They are also very good at this. Reread the section about the leather goods store. It was an ambush. Their store designer covered everything—visual, auditory, kinesthetic, and auditory digital. Your defense:

- Know your style—your filtering strengths and weaknesses.
- Have a strategy—Chapter 8.
- Have a plan—Chapter 9.
- Embrace your A. Pexx. (This can be literal; I've told clients to wear their watches on their opposite hands. The unnatural feeling kept them focused.)
- Keep your thinking brain engaged during your critical spending choices.

Money knowledge and money style complement your values and temperament. You do not need to know all the technical stuff about money to create wealth. You do need to know everything possible about how you make money choices. Remember, money is about behavior and not products and services.

KEY POINTS
- Humans are information filters.
- There are four filtering styles:

- Visual (see—eagle)
- Auditory (hear—dolphin)
- Kinesthetic (feel—elephant)
- Auditory Digital (procedures—owl)
- Know your style.
- Too much information can be overwhelming—it's just noise.
- Information is not knowledge.
- The financial industry has an owl bias.
- When working with money professionals, state your style preferences and expectations.
- Make critical spending a thinking-brain activity.

ACTION STEPS

Consider the following actions and questions, and write down your answer to each:

1. Complete the ODEE Style Inventory™.
2. Do you agree or disagree with the results? Why or why not?
3. How can your money style be an asset?
4. How can your money style be a liability?
5. Which style complements your style best? Why?
6. Which style does not complement your style? Why?

Your behavioral tool kit is complete. Now it's all about execution. Let's talk next about your money strategy.

CHAPTER EIGHT

MONEY STRATEGY

BACK AT HOME

Traffic near the mall was light for a Monday night, so it was a fast drive home. As you drive, you just can't get Juan out of your mind. You think, "Juan's party was good. It looks like he's going to be okay. He's obviously been working with the same firm as the President for some time to prepare for this. I think I need to revamp my attitude about meeting with her. What would happen to me if my job were sent overseas?" A. Pexx gently whispers, "It would not be pretty, and you know it." You shiver and ask out loud, "Is there a window open?"

When you get home, you open the fridge, look inside, and decide you aren't hungry. "I ate way too much at the party." You turn, head to the couch, and take your favorite seat in front of the television. You look at your brief case and sigh. "I need to do a few things before tomorrow." You turn on the television while grabbing a stack of papers from your brief case and sit on the couch. Looking at the pile of work, you think, "Maybe Juan is the lucky one." Your thoughts return to The Mall. "I got so flustered at the leather goods store that I forgot to stop by the book store. Oh well... I'll take a look at Dr.

Hargrove's site and see if she has something on communication." You pull out your laptop and log onto her web site. After a little searching, you find the style assessment, download it, and complete the survey. "Now I see why our presentation blew up this afternoon. According to this, I'm visual and I think the customer is auditory. Our attorney is definitely a detail guy—I think an owl. So, according to this, I was doomed as soon as I asked the attorney to build and give the presentation." You send an email to the sales manager and cancel tomorrow's meeting. "This learning style stuff looks pretty good to me. I need to do some more research. At least I now have some time to finish my book report." A. Pexx chimes in, "This stuff also works with money."

You pick up your bag and retrieve a book, along with a legal pad full of notes. Clipped to the book is a short note from the President asking you to prepare an executive summary of the book for this week's staff meeting. You pick up the book and think, "Tony Jeary. So you're the guy who got the President all fired up about strategic planning—good stuff. I'm looking forward to our retreat next month." You retrieve the summary from a folder on your computer. "Let's see; I think it's pretty complete except for one more thing." Between "Purpose" and "Core Concepts," you add:

Key Points:
Economic and social changes created by the speed of life demand a new way of strategic thinking to support and sustain the creation of superior results. If you don't get the results you desire, you will not achieve your vision. Clarity of vision with a focus on high-leverage activities produces success.

You take a few moments to read your report and smile. "I think I've got it. Strategic thinking is all about creating a clear vision, focusing on critical high-leverage tasks, and creating action steps with measurable results that everyone can get behind. I'm ready— this is going to be good. I can see us all getting behind this." SMACK! A. Pexx leans in and says, "You can use the good stuff you learn at work here at home, too—remember, you're self-employed. Boss, make the call to Tonya NOW!"

Looking at the time on your phone, you mutter, "It's too late to call tonight. Oh, I missed her call—again. But she left a voice message. Good! We're certainly playing some serious phone tag." You play her message: "This is Tonya. I know you are very busy, but I wanted to let you know that I have an opening in my schedule this Friday at 3:00. I've taken the liberty of penciling you in. If this is not going to work, please give my office a call. Unfortunately, if we can't meet on Friday, I will not have another opening until the middle of next month." You check Friday's schedule, "Late lunch at The Mall; then I'm clear for the rest of the day. I really don't feel like driving way across town on a Friday afternoon. Let's look at next month." A. Pexx, turning red with frustration, shouts, "Tonya's one of the best. You are a financial basket case—even though you don't know it. You are squandering away a fortune. You just said you need to take this more seriously. Make the appointment!" The image of Juan cutting his cake comes to mind. "On second thought, I can move lunch up an hour. Since this seems to be "Strategic Planning Month" at work, I might as well do something for myself." You make the change to your calendar, email Tonya, and save your report on Strategic Acceleration. You put away your work and turn on the television, "Dad's going to love the TV." A. Pexx moans in frustration. "At least it's on the calendar. I'll get you to the meeting!" Mall 10, You 11.

WHAT HAPPENED AFTER THE MALL?

It's finally the end of another stimulating day. All of your senses have been working overtime to filter and process trillions of bits of information—most of it meaningless static and noise. A. Pexx is proud of you—no irrational spending. Your thinking brain was much more engaged tonight than during previous trips to The Mall. A month ago, you might have bought the leather brief case. Juan's party got your attention. His "success" forced you to consider—even reframe—the consequences of potentially losing your job. He has a financial coach and a plan. You don't. This made you uncomfortable—emotionally—and made you realize that you need to change your money behavior.

You also discovered your learning style and other things from Dr. Faye's website:

- People process information and communicate through different channels.
- Effective communication happens when you provide information in a way that works with a person's individual learning style.
- Never assume everyone filters information just like you.
- Make sure your group presentations are designed for all four styles.

With a little help from A. Pexx, you also associate learning style and good money choices. Knowing how you process information and communicate will help you make better money decisions.

Writing the executive summary of Strategic Acceleration forced you to think about strategic planning. You made a logical (rational, thinking-brain) observation that the process you use at work will work at home—thank you, A. Pexx. You are self-employed and must begin to think and plan like a business owner. Finally, after some prodding, you make what might be a life-changing call to meet with a financial coach. A. Pexx is impressed, but will remain watchful—your money temperament still loves the nice stuff.

WHAT IS A MONEY STRATEGY AND
WHY DO YOU NEED ONE?

Are you still with me? It's no surprise that making good money choices is complex behavior. And given all we've covered, it's a wonder that you ever make a good money choice. Don't worry. With a first-class money strategy, it can be done. It takes some work on your part to build your strategy; but once you get started, it's easy.

Your money strategy is the grand design for your life. Since money is so important today, it's impossible to talk about your life plan and not talk about money. Like I said earlier, money is a tool—the grease of modern life. Even if your life's ambition is to give away all your stuff and live on a self-sustaining farm, you need a strategic plan.

I've been a strategic planner all my professional life—in the Marine Corps, as a financial advisor, and as a business owner with two advanced degrees in planning (now I get calls from three universities asking for money instead of just one). There are hundreds of strategic financial planning tools and techniques. Many of them are good—if you use them. And *that* is the issue. Humans don't really like to plan; and if you do the research, we aren't very good at it, either (remember the dot.com bubble; the housing bubble; and I can personally add, trying to save a few dollars by taking a military charter flight—think bus with wings—from Hawaii to New York with your 18-month-old daughter on your lap the day after you and your wife competed in the Honolulu marathon). As hard as you try to build and follow a plan (life happens, too), you may not have the temperament for it. It doesn't mean it can't be done. You just need a temperament-specific approach.

The money strategy piece of the *Money Behavior System* is just the ticket. It works with and accommodates your money temperament and style—even if you've never had a savings account, the parking attendant at The Mall knows your name and you don't even work there, even if you're never going to do a budget, even if money stuff makes your eyes cross, or even if you love money stuff and you know you know more than the pros. Do you get it? Your money strategy must reflect your money values, temperament, and knowledge in order to work. If it doesn't, you won't follow it, regardless of what you paid for your strategy. Lots of owls build financial plans for dolphins, elephants, and eagles. You don't have to be a Marlin Perkins (of Wild Kingdom fame—think Animal Planet) to know this is a problem waiting to happen. I can't tell you how many financial plans I've reviewed that were never implemented or updated because the plan did not "fit" the client's temperament and style. A great strategy with superior advice that is never followed is the same as no strategy at all—even worse, in fact, because it may create a false sense of security.

By the way, if you are building the plan with someone else, I bet they have different money values, temperament, and knowledge than you. Just a little advice: figure this all out *before* you finish your money strategy, and make sure the final plan reflects this. I've worked with people who let their spouse or partner make all the money strategy decisions — not always a good idea. (I could do an entire chapter on the dumb money choices of really smart people). Unfortunately, when—not if—these folks became "single" again, they were absolutely clueless about their money. One widow summed up this problem very succinctly after we figured out that her husband had totally fouled up their money strategy. She told me, "The difference between the dearly departed and the dead bum (she used a much stronger "b" word) is a plan." I can't say it any better than that.

Money strategy is the start of the planning process. Here is where your values, temperament, and knowledge come together with what Tony Jeary calls strategic clarity. Think of your money strategy as a vision statement for your future. It's a high-level view of everything you plan to accomplish in your life—your Big V Money Values. Your money strategy lays out the purpose and process required to get everything done. It describes what you want to do, without all the details. This is your blueprint for peace of mind in your chosen lifestyle.

Unfortunately, too many people consider strategic planning too complicated, too expensive, or only something wealthy people do—wrong on all counts. Contrary to what you think and feel, strategic planning is not all that difficult—I promise. Not planning is much more costly than planning. A good financial plan does not have to cost a fortune, and everyone needs a personal money strategy. The fact that you don't think you qualify to have a plan (not enough wealth) is exactly why you need one. A good money strategy sustains and builds wealth. Isn't that what you want?

Most people put more time and energy into planning their vacations than their retirement. Car pool "money experts" aren't going to be there for you when you have a real money issue. And as much as you scream and yell at the "talking heads" on television, they can't hear or see you. Don't you think it's strange that every month there is a new money strategy in the magazine you subscribe to? If all this information and advice were really strategic (long-term and tailored to you), it would not change daily, weekly, monthly and yearly. Tactical planning is about execution—products and services; strategic planning is about values. The common knowledge you rely on is usually tactical—a quick, easy, and "cheap" one-size-fits-all solution. This behavior creates and chases fads—tech stocks, real estate, derivatives,

IPOs, gold, and whatever was last year's winner. Your tactical money plan should always follow your strategic money plan. Now, which do you think is more important—money strategy or money tactics?

YOUR STRATEGY

What's your money strategy? Do you have one? If not, you need one. They are not difficult to build. Excluding the list below (and the few more you could probably add), you have many options. As we move forward, please try to avoid anything from the list. They are great examples of intelligent people rationalizing bad money behavior. You can do better.

- Buying lottery tickets (whether the jackpot is $10 or $10 million)
- Investing in any collectable currently being offered on cable television
- Investing in anything plated with gold or silver
- Buying any plate with a picture of Elvis, the Beatles, or a recent President
- Investing in anything that looks easy on television, at a seminar, or at a home show
- Getting involved in any job or investment offered through an unsolicited email or cold call
- Breeding or raising anything you have to feed unless you are a farmer, rancher, or licensed breeder—especially without "people" to do the nasty stuff
- Selling anything from your home that can be sold by Walmart at a lower price
- Buying or investing in anything you can't explain in your own words
- Buying or investing in anything that begins with, "I have a

friend," "This time is different," "Everyone is in this," "It's a sure thing," or "No one has ever lost money in this"

- Doing, buying, or investing in anything that does not help you achieve your critical Big V Money Values
- Doing, buying, or investing in anything that is counter to your money temperament and/or money knowledge

If any of the above listing represents your current money strategy, we need to talk—now. If any of the above was your money strategy in the past—congratulations! You now have experience. If you are working through the list until you find something that works—you are behaviorally challenged (money can make you crazy). If any of the above was once your money strategy and you have reframed and found your way—good for you! You have wisdom. If you were considering anything that looks, smells, sounds, feels, or tastes like any of the above but you stopped, thought about it, and didn't sign anything—you're a genius. Here's the cool thing about money. You can skip money experience, money stupidity, and money wisdom and go directly to money genius with a solid, long-term money strategy—it's your choice.

I mentioned Tony Jeary earlier. He's a prolific author, as well as a performance consultant, coach, and trainer to CEOs and Fortune 500 corporations. Tony knows strategic planning. I'm fortunate to have him as a strategic partner and guide. I began work on the Money Behavior System about a year before a mutual business associate introduced Tony to me. When we first talked, it was apparent that we shared common philosophies on performance—including strategic planning. We discovered that, working independently, we had developed two performance models that complemented each other. The major difference is that the Money Behavior System is a more specialized financial planning model. Strategic Acceleration, on the other hand, is a broader model suited to both individuals and organizations. Here's the point: *your money strategy is Strategic Acceleration in action*. With Tony's permission, let me show you how to develop your money strategy using the principals of Strategic Acceleration.

Strategic Acceleration has four unifying principals: speed of life, clarity, focus, and execution. Speed of life is your condition, clarity is strategic, focus is both strategic and tactical, and execution is tactical. Understanding and applying these principals will help you structure your money strategy. I've summarized Strategic Acceleration for you and added several notes (in italics) to show you how it applies to your money strategy. Check out *www.tonyjeary.com* if you'd like to learn more about Tony's work. As you read the summary, think how these points apply to you and your money—values, temperament, and knowledge.

Speed of Life (*Condition*):

- It's a global condition that presents both strategic challenges and opportunities.
- It can't be stopped, but it can be understood and leveraged.
- Knowledge and information are the cornerstone of power.
- Too much unfiltered information and choices leads to confusion and distractions (*noise*).
- Distractions (*noise*) can keep you from focusing on high-leverage critical activities.
- The challenges of modern society and the global economy demand effective leadership (*your effective leadership of your own company*).
- Leadership (*yours*) is a results contest.
- The only thing certain is uncertainty.
- Leaders (*you*) need to, "Go as far as you can see—so that you can then see farther."

Clarity (*Strategy*):

- Leaders (*you*) need a cohesive vision for sustained superior success.
- Most vision statements are unclear or difficult to articulate.
- Without clarity of vision, there is no vision.
- The leader's (*your*) clarity of vision creates the passion and commitment necessary for execution.
- A clear vision creates positive perceptions (it pulls instead of pushes).
- You must have an unambiguous view of your vision—what, where, when, and why.

Focus (*Strategy and Tactics*):

- Focus is the opposite of distraction (*noise*).
- Focus cuts through the natural clutter of modern life. *It is laser sharp.*
- *Your feeling brain is subject to noise and distractions—which is a normal state.*
- Focus is not natural—it is a learned behavior that requires practice.
- *Focus is a thinking-brain skill—it takes work.*
- The heart of the focus issue is distraction – not time management.
- Identify high-leverage activities that impact results, and focus your efforts here.

Execution (*Tactics*).

- Execution requires action.
- Leaders (*you*) must be able to persuade others to willingly embrace the vision.
- Communicating at the belief level and explaining the "why" produces a voluntary change in behavior.

- Your ability to persuade and motivate others creates in them a willingness to not only assist you, but to do so by exceeding expectations.
- Superior results require exceeding expectations daily.
- Leaders (*that's you*) who provide a positive strategic presence evoke positive cooperation.
- Leaders (*you*) must be able to communicate strategically with a positive message about your vision.

YOUR STRATEGIC MONEY STRATEGY

Remember, the rules have changed. Your condition today is different than it was a few years ago (maybe even a few seconds ago). Tony is absolutely correct; you have to move at the speed of life or you will be left standing still. Your money strategy is all about you and the business of you. The conditions you face today will be different than the conditions you face tomorrow. You must be flexible and resilient in everything you do. Before we move on, if you have not completed the action steps at the end of each chapter I recommend that you stop now and do so. (Yes, I'm talking to all of you elephants. Please turn off the television, put down the remote, and at least look at the Action Steps. Owls, thank you. I just received your typed answers—nice work.)

Assume next month's retreat is your business—you are the President. You are accountable and responsible for all outcomes—good and bad. Your task is to facilitate a business strategy session for your business. Your "job" as the leader is to energize your team to achieve the things that are important to you. Picture this message written on the white board for all of your staff to see:

> (Name of your Business)
>
> **(My) Money Strategy:**
> 1. We live and work at the speed of life.
> 2. My critical Big V Values are: (list the top 5 values)
> 3. We must overcome the following distractions in order to succeed: (list the things that can prevent success)
> 4. We have clarity of vision: (describe what success looks like)
> 5. We focus on the important : (list what needs to be done now)
> 6. Getting started is half done. A great plan that is executed with passion is better than the perfect plan that is never started.
>
> (Your signature)

Successful growing businesses (remember, this is your outcome) have clarity of vision. They know where they are going and why. Think like a business leader. Your vision statement is your highest order money value. Your vision statement is your Biggest, Most Critical, Have-to-Accomplish Money Values. (Elephants, you can't get your arms around all of this unless you have identified your Big V Values.) Do you really know what is important about money to you? You should. This is your cohesive vision of your future—your vision statement. It must be clear and emotional. It must create passion and a commitment to act. Does your critical money value generate the necessary positive pull for you to commitment to it? If it does not, you will not give up good feelings today in order to have what is important to you in the future. This is a thinking-brain activity with a feeling-brain outcome. What are you passionate about? Write it down. Shut your eyes. Envision what you will think and feel when you achieve your critical money value. Now, store that thought and those feelings somewhere in your brain, so that when the going gets tough—and it will—you can reach down and retrieve those thoughts and feelings and press on.

Next, identify the noise and distractions that will prevent you from achieving your critical money value. Success requires that you have a laser-sharp focus on what is important and learn to filter out the natural clutter of modern life. This can be difficult, because this is not your normal state (remember The Mall). Your money temperament and knowledge must be aligned with your critical money values. If your critical money value is to have financial freedom and be able to walk away from your "job" (think Juan) and open a "Worm Farm," so be it! To do this, you need to focus on the outcome—wealthy worm wrangler—and have a money strategy that will get you there. That means your money strategy must support your temperament and style, while at the same time your temperament and style support your strategy. Check your calendar and your bank statement. Do your spending and time management support your highest money values? Did you buy a vacation with your tax return while you have a large credit-card balance and no retirement plan?

To make all this work, you have to act. This is called strategic execution—putting in place a big-picture plan, along with the processes to "get it done." Think of this as your bird's-eye view of your financial plan. Here you must ask some tough questions and be very honest with yourself.

- Are my/our money values clear and unambiguous?
- Do I really know myself AND my spouse's or partner's:
  - Money temperament?
  - Money knowledge?
- Do I/we have the capacity to do this?
- Do I/we have passion for my/our critical money values—a strong why?

126

- Do I/we have the tools and resources to make it happen: time, money, education, and so on?
- Do I/we have the work processes in place? Are we in the right jobs or careers?
- Do I/we have the money systems (money products and services) in place: income, savings, investment, insurances, money team? Are they appropriate for my temperament and values?
- How will I know if I am on target?
- How will I stay motivated and engaged?

Finally, life happens very fast. Have a sense of humor and an open mind, treat everyone with dignity, and never quit.

This is the first step in a lifelong journey. Don't get all stressed out worrying about getting this first step "right" (listen up, owls). Starting is half the battle. There is no perfect strategy that is frozen in time. Your strategy will change as your life changes. The strategy you have as a young single college graduate will be different than when you marry, start a family, and decide you need a worm farm. Many people never even get this far in their life planning. Congratulations! You're already way ahead of the pack. Just reading this book and working through the exercises will help you engage your thinking brain to start planning. The planning process will help stimulate creative ideas and solution. These in turn will help your feeling brain to connect emotionally with both your critical money value and your plan to accomplish it. This beats the alternative—closing the old business, accepting less, and letting your thinking/feeling brain do the "if only" drill for the rest of your life.

You have to start. You may not get this right the first time. That's okay (listen up, owls). Do it again. Some of you may need help. That's okay, too. A money professional skilled in strategic money planning might prove invaluable. Time is your most valuable and yet scarcest resource—use it wisely on high-leverage, critical activities. A strategic plan will help you gain and maintain your freedom and dignity. If you fail to plan, you will give up your economic freedom, your ability to make money choices (trust me, someone will make these decisions for you), and your dignity. Isn't that why you bought this book in the first place? If you don't plan, you'll be 90 before you get the worm farm, if you get it at all.

KEY POINTS

- We are all moving at the speed of life.
- Success with money requires clarity of vision.
- What is most important about money to you is your most critical money value.
- Focus allows you to cut through noise and distractions.
- Successful execution of your money strategy requires clarity and focus, along with a passion for the final outcome.
- You are self-employed; treat this as a critical business activity.

ACTION STEPS

Write down—this is too important to just ask—how you think and feel about each of the following questions:

1. What are your highest priority Big V money values?
2. Will it require money to achieve or satisfy these values?
3. Do you have the money now?
4. Will you have the money in the future (inflation adjusted)? How and why?
5. What is your money temperament?
6. What is your money knowledge and learning style?

7. Are your money values aligned with your money temperament and knowledge?
8. Do you currently have a money strategy?
9. If you have a strategic money strategy, what is it?
10. Is it working? Why or why not?
11. Write out your money strategy.

With your new money strategy on paper and a passion for what is important about money to you; it's time to write your action plan.

CHAPTER 9

MONEY ACTION

THE MEETING

It's Friday, you've had a good week. Thanks to Dr. Faye, you now have a happy customer, the staff meeting went well, and now you're looking forward to your meeting with Tonya. As you enter Tonya's office, A. Pexx perks up and says, "Okay, eagle eye, this is an important meeting. Tonya is going to do some needed financial triage. You're gonna need some clarity and focus to get through this. That's what I'm all about, so I'll be running the meeting." You quickly scan the office. It's very nice—professional, but not over-the-top. A. Pexx notes, "Looks like she knows what she's doing." The receptionist greets you and escorts you to Tonya's office. A. Pexx approves and comments, "Right on schedule and no waiting. I like that."

As you go in, A. Pexx firmly whispers, "Put your game face on. I'm in charge, so listen to me. Commit to nothing—don't sign anything." You mentally inspect the office and smile in approval, "Good. No love-me wall, sales awards, or similar stuff the last person I saw was so proud of. It appears she is more interested in my retirement than her retirement. We're off to a good start." You shake hands and take a seat. After a few minutes of small talk and "who do you know" Tonya leans forward and says, "I'm very passionate about what I do.

My goal today is for us to get to know each other and determine if we have a basis to do business. I want to get to understand how you think and feel about money. I also want to help you identify what makes money important to you—the role money plays in your life."
A. Pexx starts jumping up and down, arms waving, "I told you she was good! Stay focused." Tonya continues, "After that, and if we both agree, we will determine how best to work together." She pauses and asks, "What are your expectations of our meeting today?"

You think to yourself, "Wait! What just happened? Where's the 20-minute speech about how great she is and all the spectacular things she's done for her clients and what she can do for me? I think I like where this is going."

As Tonya asks, "What are your expectations for today's meeting?" You think, "A. Pexx, help me here. That's not the question I expected." A. Pexx smugly leaves you on your own. You pause, gather your thoughts, and say, "A number of people I respect referred me to you. I simply want to learn more about you and how you work with your clients—your philosophy and approach." Then without thinking you add, "I've been doing this myself for some time, and I think I'm pretty good at it. I'm also working with a couple of other people in town." A. Pexx starts looking for the duct tape to put over your mouth. "Doing this yourself??? What makes you think you know what you're doing? Yeah, you took an economics course in school and you have an online investment account, but look at the numbers—oh yeah, I forgot. You don't like to look at the numbers. You like the pictures. Econ 101 has nothing to do with personal finance, and you're so busy at work you don't even have time to open your statements. You haven't even followed up with the HR Department to change your benefits like you said you were going to do. As for your 'people,' I don't believe your brother-in-law and your old roommate qualify." Tonya smiles and asks, "You want to know how I think and feel about money and, if it is appropriate, how we might work together. Is that correct?" Without thinking you blurt out, "Of course... yes." A. Pexx begins to pace while trying to concentrate on Tonya's every word.

Tonya then asks, "What are your expectations of me?" A. Pexx nods in approval, commenting, "Wow, this girl is first-rate." You think again and say, "Good question. Nobody has ever asked that one before. Let's see: I'm smart, I'm busy, and I have a good career. I used to be able to do this all by myself." A. Apexx mouths, "Yeah, right!" "I think my biggest challenge now is just finding the time to do it all by myself. Between work and all the things I volunteer with, I don't have enough time to deal with all this stuff and still have a life. I simply am not able to keep up with all the information like I used to. I need someone I trust who can help me cut through all the garbage and help me focus on what is important—to me. I also expect you to be honest with me. I hate to be patronized. If I'm heading in the wrong direction, I expect you to tell me. (A. Pexx, gives a big thumbs up and says, "That's why you dropped your first money guy and opened an online account."). Finally, I need good communication. I don't expect you to be available 24/7, but at least answer my calls within a reasonable time—24 hours. I also think you should take the time to find out the things that are important to me and how I think and feel about money. I'm not here to be sold anything." You laugh. "Oh, and making me some money would also be nice."

A. Pexx smiles approvingly and gushes, "Good for you! It's working; I think you are finally starting to get it about money. Like I say, it's all about what's between your ears."

Tonya smiles and continues to take notes. She looks up and says, "I think you will like our process. Is there anything else?" A. Pexx sits down and confidently begins to monitor the conversation.

Tonya then puts her pen down, looks you in the eye, and says, "I think it is also important for you to know what I expect of you."

A. Pexx perks up and with a stunned look says to you, "I've never heard that from anyone before! I guess she isn't just a glorified sales clerk—and that's a good thing." Tonya continues, "I expect you to be honest and open with me. The advice I provide you is only as good as the information and data you provide me. Do not expect more of me than the information you provide. I'm not very good at reading minds; so if you ever have a question or concern, please let me know. I am passionate about helping my clients get what is important in life to them. I also know that you don't read minds. So if I say something or do something that does not make sense to you, or if I use a word you are not familiar with, please stop me so I can explain. If you can't explain in your own words why I've made a recommendation or why you own a product or service, I haven't done my job. I also understand that I have to earn your trust and that this may take some time. And I assume that someone of your stature is currently working with other money professionals. That's fine. And we will work at your pace."

You are starting to feel really comfortable with Tonya when A. Pexx stands up and says, "Ask her about where she thinks the economy is going and what she'd recommend that you do." Before you can ask the question, Tonya adds, "I'm a coach or consultant—not an analyst. My job is not to predict where the economy is going—I don't know. My job is to help you avoid catastrophic mistakes with your money. I do this by helping you identify and understand your money behavior. I'd rather help you design a money strategy that works with your behavior than 'sell' you something that doesn't fit and then have to deal with your behavior. Does that make sense to you?" A. Pexx starts to jump up and down and shouts, "She gets it! She gets it! I hope you are listening!"

You say, "Let me get this straight. You're going to try to figure out my relationship with money. Good luck. You might not like what you find." A. Apexx leans in and whispers, "Listen up! You might learn something."

Tonya chuckles and says, "What we do here is really pretty simple. Let me walk you through the Money Belief System." Your mind says, "I'm listening." But your body language says, "I'm confused." You speak up and skeptically say, "This sounds so different. How come I've never heard of anything like this before?"

Tonya leans forward and says with confidence, "Let me explain. We believe that money success has more to do with your behavior than the products and services you own. We think that if we can help you identify and understand your money behavior, you will make better money decisions."

You respond, "Okay. That makes sense. How does this work?"

Tonya continues, "First I will help you identify your money values. I want to know why money is important to you. I need to understand about the things that are important in your life that require money."

You nod and A. Pexx chimes in with, "Does this sound familiar?"

"Then I will have you log onto our web site and take a temperament profile. I will use the results to learn how you think and feel about money and your learning style. Knowing these things about you will help me design a money strategy that better fits your money behavior."

You interject, "Okay, in my own words: My money temperament is how I think and feel about money. And how I think and feel about money influences how I spend my money. So, if I build a plan around my temperament, I should have a better handle on my spending. If my spending is under control, I can save and invest more." A. Pexx gives you a thumbs up and says, "Yes! That's how you decorated your office and how Juan planned for his future. This will work for you. Pay attention."

Tonya nods and says, "I think you have the idea."

You continue, "Then you will build a financial plan around my behavior. The plan should work better, because it's based on my temperament."

Tonya adds, "That's right. Your money strategy will reflect your money behavior. I will then select products and services that support your strategy."

As her plan sinks in, you nod your head in agreement and say, "You'll recommend money stuff that fits my money strategy. Hmmm, and since my money strategy is based on how I think and feel about money, this should all work better for me—because it is all designed around me and for me." Then, feeling A. Pexx's approval, you ask, "How come no one else does this? I mean, it just makes sense. We build human behavior into everything else we do—why not money? I guess this also means that if we work together to do all this, I should have more time and less stress."

Tonya and A. Pexx smile and you ask, "What do we do next?" Tonya responds, "I need to get some background information, ask a few basic questions about your current financial situation, talk about your money values, and identify a few critical financial goals. Then we will talk about how you and I will work together. Finally, depending on how we decide to work together, I'll give you some homework to complete before our next meeting. How does that sound to you?" You and A. Pexx do a virtual high five. "Great!"A. Pexx shouts, "The eagle has landed. This is one step for..."

It takes Tonya about half an hour to collect the rest of the information she needs, and then you two discuss how you would like to work together. After she explains your homework, she looks up, puts her pen down, and asks, "What questions do you have?"

You think for a moment and ask, "So, based on what you know so far, do you have any recommendations for my money?" Tonya *smiles and says, "I have some ideas, but it is too early to say until I review your money behavioral profile. Remember, it's behavior then products—not products then behavior."*

Tonya sets your next meeting, makes sure you have your to-do list, and gives you a few business cards, explaining that she works exclusively by referral. As you turn to leave you say, "My dad will be here next week. If you like a challenge, you need to meet him. Are you interested?" Tonya says, "Sure. Give me a call when they get in, and we'll talk." As you turn to leave, you see Jenny Miller sitting in an office with another advisor. With a feeling of great satisfaction, you think, "I get it now." A. Pexx does a double back flip and smiles. New game: Mall 0, You 0.

IT WAS A GOOD MEETING

The meeting with Tonya went well—A. Pexx is elated. The meeting was the culmination of a number of events and discoveries that caused you to reframe your money beliefs. Your old belief set was, "I can do it all myself. I'm smart, there is plenty of information on money; all I have to do is pick the right products and services (the common wisdom about money), and everything will work out." Your new belief set is, "I'm in charge, but I can't do it all by myself. My money success is all about my money behavior (values, temperament, and knowledge). The many money products and services available to me are simply tools to help me execute my money plan." The meeting worked because Tonya listened, established expectations, and focused on your behavior, and she did not simply try to sell you products and services. It was also a good meeting because you were ready to have the meeting. As good as Tonya is, if you were not emotionally ready for a change, the meeting would not have been successful. Once you began to question your established money beliefs and the common wisdom, you opened yourself up to a different approach; and you discovered that the *Money Belief System* fits your new money beliefs.

MONEY ACTION IS TACTICAL

Money action is the last phase of the Money Behavior System. This phase is all about taking the necessary steps to execute your money strategy. This is the transition step from planning to doing. By now, you should have a good idea about your money behavior profile—who you are, what you want to do, and your money strategy. What remains is a plan to put the critical behaviors and activities into motion—it's time to get it done. Also, I need to point out that this is where most traditional personal finance and money books start. I guess by now you know that I think a little differently than most money pros about money. It's all about you and not the stuff. I could have easily added another ten chapters on techniques, products, and services. I chose not to do so, because there are thousands of excellent books, courses, and web sites devoted to this stuff. They all complement this book well. I think you are capable of finding one that will fit your newly found money belief profile. However, in deference to those who feel you need some tactical "how to" guidance—and to prove that I do, in fact, know and use this stuff—here goes.

Accepted financial planning practice standards acknowledge six steps in the financial planning process (see, this already sounds stuffy). Your action plan should follow these steps. Step 1 assumes you are working with a financial professional. Steps 2, 3, 4, 5, and 6 need to be done by everyone (but you know my bias on doing this yourself).

1. Define the relationship between you and the money pro. What are your expectations? How will the pro get paid? What products and/or services will you receive? How can

the relationship be modified or stopped? What does a positive outcome look like? Do you both agree?

2. Define your financial goals and objectives and collect information. What are your personal financial needs, wants, and goals, by priority? When do you want to achieve them? What is your current financial situation? What information and documentation do you have to support your current financial situation?

3. Analyze and evaluate your current financial situation. Identify all cash flows, assets, and liabilities. Do you have a budget? How does it look? What do you own? What do you owe? What is your net worth? Review taxes. Conduct risk assessment and survivor needs analysis (a comprehensive insurance review). Review all benefits and entitlements. Review retirement plans. Review all estate planning documents—your will, trusts, and related paperwork. Review all business documents. Conduct a suitability review of all financial instruments, products, and services. Conduct a financial goals analysis.

4. Develop a financial plan to achieve your financial goals and satisfy your critical needs. Do you have a financial plan? Is it current? Is it comprehensive? Identify and evaluate financial planning solutions—products and services.

5. Implement your financial plan. Select the appropriate products and services. Write out your implementation plan. Include explicit responsibilities and all associated costs. What are you going to do? Who is going to do it? What is it going to cost?

6. Monitor the plan and collect feedback. Who is going to monitor what? What are your metrics? What does

success look like? Who provides feedback, and to whom? When will reviews be conducted? What triggers a change to the plan? Who will make the change? What will it cost to make a change—in taxes, fees, and commissions?

This is very important stuff—that most people never do. Mess any of this up, and money will really drive you crazy. I could go on for pages about this stuff—but I won't do that here. The financial services industry is massive, complex, and sophisticated. If you want to go down that road, and I encourage you to always learn more about money, go for it. But before you begin, think about what you thought and felt when you read the six steps of the accepted financial planning process. Based on what you now know about your learning style and temperament, how did you filter and process each step and requirement? What did your mind see, hear, feel and sense? Did you want to jump in or run away? Your response—what you felt and what you thought—is your money behavior profile as it relates to money action. A few people are wired to do all of this. Some are wired to do some of this. And a lot of people are wired to do none of this. Be honest—which are you?

Here is one of the most frustrating things about money action and why trying to do all of this makes you so crazy. Everyone— government, boss, spouse, partner, kids, educators, and friends— assumes not only that you *can* do this but that you *will* do this. Now, how's that working out for you? Most people's heads start to hurt when they look at the list, to say nothing of actually executing it. You can have all the clarity and focus in the world, but if your temperament and learning style are not suited to the task, you will not do it. This is why trying to do everything yourself is so difficult. Then add the reality of the speed of life—I think you get it.

This is why I'm not attempting to provide you with an action plan with products and services. I can't. I don't know you. If I don't know your money behavior profile, how can I possibly recommend a specific money action plan? You are unique. You deserve a unique money solution. A one-size-fits-all plan can provide general direction and focus. It might even be suited in some circumstances—if you are young, just getting started, and have the basic requirements. But beyond that, you need more. Here is your money dilemma: you have more money choices than ever before. You are more responsible for the outcome of your money choices than ever before. *You have to know how you make your money choices in order for you to make better money choices.* And no one is talking about this very much.

KEY POINTS

- Money action is tactical—it's all about executing your plan.
- Money action is the "how" that follows the "why" in the Money Behavior System.
- Money action can be complex or simple, depending on your condition or situation.
- Money action uses your thinking brain during planning and your feeling brain during execution—without emotion, the plan will not work.
- The common wisdom about money focuses on activity, products, and services, and not behavior.
- Your money behavior profile will dictate the type and quality of your action plan.
- You are accountable and responsible for your action plan—regardless of the quality of the plan.
- A quality action plan conforms to the six steps of the Financial Planning Process.
- Money professionals can help in all or part of the process required for developing and executing your plan.

ACTION STEPS

Ask yourself, or better yet, write down your answer to each of the following questions:

1. Do you have a comprehensive money action plan?
2. Who developed it?
3. Is it current?
4. Is it funded, and are you following it? Why or why not?
5. Does it reflect your money behavior profile?
6. Do you understand each component of your plan? Can you explain it in plain language?
7. Who else knows about your plan? If anything happened to you, could they take over?
8. How do you measure success?
9. How often do you review your plan?
10. What would cause you to change your plan? Why?

It's time to head back to The Mall to see how well this is all working.

CHAPTER 10

NOW I GET IT

You are sitting in your office going over your notes when you receive a text message from Tonya. It reads, "Your dad just left. He's still on track. Call for details." You stare at the message and think, "If anyone could get dad on track and keep him there, it's Tonya. I can't believe it's been a year since we started working together. Best decision I ever made." A. Pexx perks up, and with a very I-get-no-respect look says, "Thanks! I wasn't along just for the ride. Without me, you'd still be on the cruise." You think, "Mom and I will have our sanity back. No more crazed calls about losing money—there were paper losses—or how smart he is when he wins one. Now all I have to tell him is, 'Call Coach Tonya.'"

You put down your phone and think about how much better you feel now that you are working with Tonya. "I now have a solid money strategy and action plan—written specifically for me. It's so nice not to have to deal with all the distraction and stress of doing everything myself. I can't believe I waited so long to do this!" A. Pexx chimes in with, "It is what it is. Flush that thought. You're now on track."

On your tablet you jot down the following list:

"Now I Get It!"

- I like the Money Behavior System...
- Get more of Tonya's business cards to hand out to friends

- *Schedule program review for next month*
- *Less money stress...*
- *Fewer money distractions...*
- *More clarity and focus on what's important to me*
- *Written financial plan—that I actually understand*
- *Cash flow under control*
- *No credit card debt; stupid spending under control—most of the time (keep on it)*
- *Six months emergency savings—half-way there... delayed gratification is OK (work in progress)*
- *Retirement plan reallocated, funded, and on track*
- *Insurance reviewed and updated*
- *Know my money behavior profile—SPENDER!!!!*
- *Made a friend*
- *Not afraid to delegate money stuff*
- *My business is—SWEET AND GETTING BETTER EVERY DAY!!*

Life is good... and A. Pexx smiles, bows, and continues to sign autographs.

The alarm on your phone goes off and you take a quick look. "Wow, if I don't leave now, I'll be late for lunch with Jenny at her place at The Mall. Gotta run." You put on your coat and head to your car. As you close your door, you catch a glimpse of your reflection in a window. "Hmmm, this old coat looks good. I wouldn't have thought so last year at this time." You smile and push the button for the elevator. As the elevator descends to the parking garage, you think, "I can't remember the last time I was at The Mall. I guess it's been about six months." And A. Pexx chimes in with, "Yeah, you used to live here. It's amazing what can happen when you take the time to lay out your money values. And don't forget, I found you Tonya; well, at least I got you to the first appointment."

When you park your car at The Mall, you do a quick mental check list—just like an airline pilot. A. Pexx follows along as you go through your list. "Let's see, go directly to Jenny's—don't stop anywhere (check). If I see anything along the way that I think I can't live without that costs more than $50.00, make a note—don't look or touch (check). Cash and debit card only (check). And leave the flyer with the coupons to the Big Expensive Department Store in the car (check). Let's go." A. Pexx gives a big "thumbs up," and says, "Roger, ready to launch."

As A. Pexx scurries ahead clearing the way, you move rapidly to Jenny's, not really "looking" at what is going around you. A. Pexx yells, "Keep moving—hup, two, three, four... Looking good!"

Jenny is waiting for you in the room where Juan had his party. During the last year, the two of you have become good friends. A. Pexx, never one to be overly modest, takes all the credit for that too. You smile and say to Jenny, "I'm looking forward to taste-testing your new menu today. Can we start with dessert?"

After an hour of calories, stories, and laughs, your phone alarm sounds. "Jenny, I've had a ball. I wish I had something fun like this at work that I could share with you. I know! How about joining us at the theater next month? We're one of the corporate sponsors—back stage passes!" For some reason, the thought of a $50.00 t-shirt pops into your mind and you think, "I wonder where that shirt went? I'm definitely not going to do that this year." And A. Pexx bows.

As you are returning to your car, you stop by a display for the new "THING." A. Pexx begins to panic. You pick up a flyer and begin to study the new features and benefits. A. Pexx starts to rapidly pace back and forth. Your heart rate begins to rise, your eyes widen, and you feel a little flush. "Wow, this looks so cool. I wonder how much it costs." Immediately a clerk approaches you with a clipboard and explains, "We are the first store in the region to have the new version of the "THING." In fact, the demand is so great that we are taking advance orders. Only a very select number of customers will have the opportunity to purchase the new version." A. Pexx begins to feel ill. "In view of our exclusive position with the manufacturer, I am authorized to offer you the new version at an exclusive price." You start to salivate and think, "These new features are unbelievable. I need this." The clerk smiles, and in anticipation of a sale says, "Shall I reserve one for you with your Mall card? If you act now I am authorized to waive all shipping charges." A. Pexx is now in full blown arrest and screams, "NOOOOOOOOOOOOOOOOOOO.... "You calmly reach into your pocket while A. Pexx starts looking for the "white flag." From your pocket, you retrieve one of Tonya's pens. You look at the pen, and then you look at the clerk, smile, and take the clip board. With no emotion, you copy down the web site information and all the relevant contact information. Then you calmly hand the clipboard back to the clerk, return the pen to your pocket, and leave. A. Pexx shows signs of life and whispers, "That was close."

As you walk to your car, you give A. Pexx a high-five. You see a complete stranger and say with a huge smile, "I get it now! I know the prescription—do you?"

KEY POINTS

Taking the time and effort to build your money behavior profile might just be the prescription you need to cure your money insanity. Money is too important to get wrong. There is seldom a do-over. The older you get, the harder it is for you to recover from your money mistakes. Take control of your financial future now. Use the Money Behavior System. It will help you make better money choices.

You (and your A. Pexx) have a challenge. Managing money today has never been more challenging. Human nature and the common wisdom about money conspire to take you off task. You live in a consumer-driven economy that is changing at the speed of life. Add to this the fact that today everyone is self-employed. You are in charge. You are responsible and accountable for a multi-million-dollar enterprise—your household. Do the math; if you work for 40 years and average $75,000 per year over that period—that's $3,000,000! Not considering inflation and all that techie stuff (oh yeah, and life happens), that's still a fair chunk of change. So run your life like a business, and don't squander your time and money on the unimportant. With all the opportunity and money tools available today, you'd think as a society we'd be better at this. We aren't—because we are human. And money drives us crazy.

I've given you a system to help you make better money choices. It works, and it will work for you—if you use it. The power of the Money Behavior System is its simplicity—a money strategy built around your behavior instead of trying to change your behavior to fit a strategy. Hey, I'm a simple guy—make it too complicated, and it won't work (Marine-proof solution).

THE MONEY BEHAVIOR SYSTEM

- Humans are not wired to work well with money; therefore, money makes us crazy.
  - It's your biology—how you think and feel about money
  - It's your culture—consumption and information
  - It's your belief systems—your limiting and enabling beliefs about money
  - It's the rules of money—changing at the speed of life
- Money decisions are not always rational (humans are emotional)
  - Know your money values—what is most important about money to you

- Know your money temperament—how you think and feel about money
- Know you money knowledge—how you filter and process information
- Know your money strategy—clarity and focus
- Know you money action—high-leveraged execution
- Repeat until you get it right

Here's a disclaimer: I'm biased. I think you need a money coach. At least when your situation becomes so complex and crazy that doing it yourself does more real and emotional harm than it helps. I can't tell you when this will happen to you, but it usually does at some point. When you hit the point you think you need help—you do. Don't fight the inclination. I've worked with too many people that didn't realize they were in over their heads until it was too late. Those are not happy meetings, and they can be avoided. I agree that there are some people who are very good with money and are able to do everything themselves, but I think they are a minority. And as you now know, they have the money behavior for it. The question is, "Do you?"

To me, a money professional is someone with a license (when required) to sell financial products and services and/or give advice on financial products and services in exchange for compensation—wage, commissions, and/or fees. They can work in banking, insurance, securities, advisory services, or any combination. To me, character, experience, and reputation are more important than education, training, designations, and certifications. I think you need to find a pro with a good track record with people, or one who works on a team with a good track record with people. You need a pro who "gets it." Tonya gets it. You need to find your Tonya. You'll know you have the right someone when the discussion is all about you and how you think and feel about money. You want a money coach who is passionate about helping you get the things that are important to you in life. The people who need to sell you something may not necessarily be bad people. You just need to ask yourself if their solution fits your strategy. In this case, you are buying the product or service—not the coaching. You need to know the difference. Here's the bottom line: money coaches can be essential to your ultimate financial success. Think of your money coach as a person who is serving on your board of directors. You get what you hire. Make sure that whoever you hire is a good fit for you—think behavior first, then products and services. Take your time to choose; this is an important relationship that could last generations. If you've ever been to Texas, you might have heard this expression: "All hat—no cows." Be careful that you don't buy just the hat when you need the cows.

As I stated at the beginning of the book, I've been working with people and money all of my life. And the longer I work with people and money, the more I believe that financial success, wealth, and emotional happiness are all about behavior. The products and services you happen to own along the way simply leverage your time and your money. But the products themselves have little to do with your ultimate success (there are times when you are just lucky and hit the jackpot with something—but never confuse luck with brilliance). Here's an interesting list of things I've picked up about money that you might want to consider as you gaze into the future with your checkbook in hand:

- You can't time the market, so don't try.
- Stuff happens—often randomly—so know the risks and prepare accordingly.
- Given enough data you can "prove" anything; numbers folks don't always do numbers well, and it requires a computer(s) to really muddle things up.

- It takes a committee to build things that cost a lot and don't work very well; beware of group think.
- Numbers scare us. You like a good story more than a long spread sheet (beware of the sales presentation with no numbers that puts your feeling brain some place you can't afford).
- You can find data, numbers, and experts to support any position you take with your money. Don't try to prove the wisdom of your money choice; instead, try to prove it's a dumb idea (I just ask my wife).
- Our minds like order and patterns—twelve months of great performance in a stock or mutual fund may, in fact, mean nothing.
- Just because you saw it does not make it true (your analysis of the twelve months of great performance...)
- You like to trust experts—even when they aren't.
- You are not as smart as you think; just because you are good at one thing does not mean you are good at something else (listen up, really smart professional people).
- Even though our brains like to make thing simple and orderly, some stuff is just hard and complex.
- Given enough time you can rationalize anything—and you will.
- You love your stuff—and it's worth more than anyone else's.
- The financial media are the experts and have your interest at heart—sometimes…
- Money makes us crazy and it always will—but it *can* be managed.
- You have coaches for everything else you do; is money any less important than yoga, skiing, golf…?
- It's all about your behavior; embrace your money profile

and adapt. You'll be happier—and in the long run, potentially wealthier.

- Head to The Mall—it's a working laboratory on money behavior.

Now I have to go. There's a bike sale at The Mall... THUMP! That's the sound of A. Pexx hitting the floor. I think I hear him saying, "Back to work! My job never ends!"

THE MONEY BEHAVIOR SYSTEM™

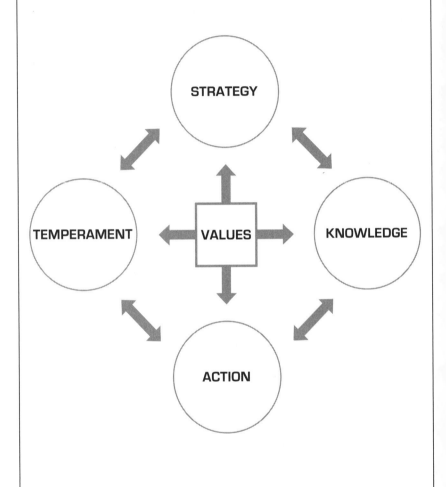

"ONE SIZE FITS ONE . . ."

ODEE STYLE INVENTORY™

Your answers on this inventory will help you understand how you learn, organize, remember and speak about your experiences of the world. There are no "*right*" or "*wrong*" answers. Read each question carefully and indicate your answer based on the instructions given in each section. Do not spend too much time thinking about any one question.

1. **Consider what each word or phrase means. Choose the one in each group that appeals _most_ to you. Select only one word per group.**

   a.) ○ melody   b.) ○ make contact
        ○ passion   ○ visualize
        ○ process   ○ sequence
        ○ appearance   ○ tune in

   c.) ○ conversation   d.) ○ look
        ○ logic   ○ grasp
        ○ gut feelings   ○ analyze
        ○ the big picture   ○ sounds like

2. **Mark *T* or *F* based on whether the following statements apply to you _most_ of the time.**

   a. _____ I *often* depend on my gut feelings and intuition when making decisions.

   b. _____ I pay close attention to the tone and sound of people's voices.

c. _____ When assembling an object such as a toy or a piece of furniture, I prefer to work from the diagram and see the end result.

d. _____ I can follow directions *best* if I can hear them read or told to me.

e. _____ I learn *best* by doing.

f. _____ When making decisions I am guided more by logic and facts than by the way an idea sounds or makes me feel.

g. _____ If I want to remember a phone number, I picture it in my mind then I write it down.

h. _____ Facts and figures appeal to me more than feelings and sounds.

i. _____ I am a really good listener.

3. **Circle the letter beside the phrase you are _most likely_ to use.**
   a. I see what you mean.
   b. Do you hear what I'm saying?
   c. It just doesn't feel right.
   d. That makes perfect sense.

4. **I follow instructions for putting together a toy or a piece of furniture _best_ if** *(circle one)*
   a. someone can read the instructions to me as I work
   b. the instructions are presented in a picture or diagram
   c. I can lay out the pieces and get a feel for how they connect
   d. the instructions make sense and follow a logical sequence and flow

5. **Which of the following statements describes most how you like to learn about a new technique?** *(circle one)*

   a. I like to know how and why it works.

   b. Let me listen to you explain it.

   c. Show me a diagram, picture or model.

   d. Walk me through it or demonstrate it for me.

6. **Which statement _best_ describes you?** *(circle one)*

   a. If you want me to remember something, you better write it down, send me an email or give me a note!

   b. I enjoy facts and figures and making sense of them.

   c. I have to get a good feeling about an idea before I can accept it.

   d. I would rather listen to a speaker first and take notes later, if I need to.

ODEE STYLE INVENTORY™
SCORE SHEET

Your answers on this inventory will help you understand how you learn, organize, remember and speak about your experiences of the world. Remember, there are no "right" or "wrong" answers or styles. To compute your score, compare your responses to each item to the corresponding key below. Record one point for every item in the appropriate Score Box cell. For example, if you chose "melody" for item 1a, give yourself 1 point in the Score Box cell labeled "Dolphin Auditory (A)."

1. In the box next page give yourself one point for each answer that corresponds to the item you circled.

   a.) A-melody
       K-passion
       AD-process
       V-appearance

   b.) K-make contact
       V-visualize
       AD-sequence
       A-tune in

   c.) A-conversation
       AD-logic
       K-gut feelings
       V-the big picture

   d.) V-look
       K-grasp
       AD-analyze
       A-sounds like

2. Record a point in the appropriate box next page *only* if you answered *"T"* to that item. For example, if you chose marked

"T" for item 2a, give yourself 1 point in the box labeled "Elephant Kinesthetic E."

a. <u>K</u>   d. <u>A</u>   g. <u>V</u>

b. <u>A</u>   e. <u>K</u>   h. <u>AD</u>

c. <u>V</u>   f. <u>AD</u> i. <u>A</u>

3. Record one point in the appropriate box below for each answer that corresponds to the item you circled.

3.		4.		5.		6.	
a.	<u>V</u>	d.	<u>A</u>	g.	<u>AD</u>	g.	<u>V</u>
b.	<u>A</u>	e.	<u>V</u>	h.	<u>A</u>	h.	<u>AD</u>
c.	<u>K</u>	f.	<u>K</u>	i.	<u>V</u>	i.	<u>K</u>
a.	<u>AD</u>	d.	<u>AD</u>	g.	<u>K</u>	g.	<u>A</u>

Total the points in each box. The highest score is your primary ODEE Style. The second highest score is **your secondary ODEE Style.**

SCORE BOX

	OWL Auditory Digital (AD)	DOLPHIN Auditory (A)	ELEPHANT Kinesthetic (K)	EAGLE Visual (V)	ODEE STYLE*
Score					(Highest Score)
Totals					

*Ties are not unusual

(Note: The *ODEE Style Inventory*™ was developed by C. LaFaye Hargrove, PhD and Cherry Collier, PhD based on the principles of Neurolinguistic Programming.)

ODEE STYLE INVENTORY™
REPORT

The **ODEE Styles**™ represent four basic approaches to how you use your brain and senses to process and communicate information. Your **ODEE Style**™ describes ways in which you learn, organize, remember and speak about your experiences of the world. Every moment of every day, you are bombarded with massive amounts of information. It is physically impossible to register everything you see, hear, feel and think simultaneously. Your mind uses your senses and filtering systems to store and recall information in such as way that it takes note of what it thinks is important and deletes the rest.

While you use all five senses, most people tend to lean primarily on one or two filtering systems to take in information and communicate meaning about what is experienced. The inventory measures the style you prefer to use *most* of the time. You may also have traits from other styles or use others styles depending upon the situation. It is not unusual to demonstrate different styles on different occasions.

YOUR PRIMARY ODEE STYLE™ IS:

OWL Owls seek order and want to make sense of their world. Attention to detail and wanting to know exactly why things are the way they are is one common characteristic of Owls. They like information. They memorize by steps, procedures and sequences. They look for rational explanations, think logically and seek logical answers, facts and data. When making decisions, Owls are more likely to accept an idea or proposal when something has been measured, categorized, analyzed, or quantified in some way. Questions they frequently ask are: *"Does it make sense?" "How long will it take and how much will it cost?"* Owls may spend a fair amount of time talking to themselves.

DOLPHIN Dolphins relate most effectively to sounds and the spoken word. They understand new ideas and concepts best when they hear the information. They are easily distracted by noise. Dolphins have a remarkable ability to repeat back what you tell them, word for word. They learn best when they can concentrate on the words and tone of voice of the speaker. They will tend to listen to a speaker and then take notes afterwards. Often information written down will have little meaning until it has been heard. A Dolphin might say *"I can't hear myself think!"* or *"Do you hear what I'm saying?"*

ELEPHANT Elephants experience the world through feelings, touch, movement and space. They learn skills by imitation and practice. They are intuitive. Before accepting an idea, an elephant must *get a feel* for what they are doing. They use body language to communicate and may touch people when they talk to them. Elephants can typically do more than one thing at a time and may get bored if required to sit for long periods of time. They would rather play sports or do a craft than sit still and read a book. They tend to be physically active and enjoy the outdoors. An Elephant might say *"I can't put my finger on it but my gut tells me something isn't quite right."*

EAGLE Eagles rely primarily on their sense of sight to take in information, understand, and remember it. If they don't "see" it, they're not able to fully comprehend it. Eagles relate most effectively to written information, notes, diagrams and pictures. They memorize by seeing pictures.. To an extent, information does not exist for an Eagle unless they can see it written down or in a diagram. Eagles are very good at working with colors and pictures, and using the "mind's eye". They are usually neat and organized and good note-takers. An Eagle might ask, *Do you see what I'm saying?*

YOUR SECONDARY ODEE STYLE™ IS:

○ OWL   ○ DOLPHIN   ○ ELEPHANT   ○ EAGLE

You can identify another person's ODEE Style by listening to the words they chose.

EAGLE Visual (V)	DOLPHIN Auditory (A)	ELEPHANT Kinesthetic (K)	OWL Auditory Digital (AD)
Memorize by seeing pictures. They are interested by how the program looks. Are bored by long verbal instructions because their mind may wander	They can repeat things back to you easily & learn by listening. Tone of voice and the words used can be important.	They memorize by doing or walking through something. They will be interested in a program that feels right or gives them a gut feeling.	They memorize by steps, procedures, sequences. They will want to know the program makes sense. They can also exhibit characteristics of other styles.

EAGLE Visual (V)	**DOLPHIN** Auditory (A)	**ELEPHANT** Kinesthetic (K)	**OWL** Auditory Digital (AD)
see	hear	feel	sense
look	listen	touch	experience
view	sound(s)	grasp	understand
appear	make music	get hold of	think
show	harmonize	slip through	learn
dawn	tune in/out	catch on	process
reveal	be all ears	tap into	decide
envision	rings a bell	make contact	motivate
illuminate	silence	throw out	consider
imagine	be heard	turn around	change
clear	resonate	hard	perceive
foggy	deaf	unfeeling	insensitive
focused	mellifluous	concrete	distinct
hazy	dissonance	scrape	conceive
crystal	question	get a handle	know
picture	unhearing	solid	

STANDARD CLOSING PHRASES REWORKED FOR ODEE STYLE

EAGLE Visual (V)	**DOLPHIN** Auditory (A)	**ELEPHANT** Kinesthetic (K)	**OWL** Auditory Digital (AD)
If I could **SHOW** you an **ATTRACTIVE** way to improve your team's performance, you would at least want to **LOOK** at it, wouldn't you? If this **LOOKS GOOD** to you we will go ahead and **FOCUS** on getting the paperwork in.	If I could **TELL** you a way in which you could improve your team's performance, you would at least want to **HEAR** about it, wouldn't you? If this **SOUNDS GOOD** to you we will go ahead and **DISCUSS** how to set up an account.	If I could help you **GET HOLD** of a **CONCRETE** way in which you could improve your team's performance, you would at least want to **GET A FEEL FOR IT**, wouldn't you? If this **FEELS GOOD** to you we will go ahead & set up an account by **HANDLING** the paperwork.	If I could help you **KNOW** how to **CHANGE** your operations so you would **EXPERIENCE** improved team performance, you would at least want to **CONSIDER IT**, wouldn't you? If this **MAKES SENSE** to you we will go ahead and get the paperwork **PROCESSED**.

ABOUT THE AUTHOR

I think you should know something about my story. I doubt that I'm all that different from you when it comes to money. Like you, I'm human. Therefore, I make human mistakes with money. As a result, money drives me crazy and at times has made me a bit stupid. Just ask my wife; she's been keeping score for years.

I grew up in a small town in upstate New York. It was a Norman Rockwell kind of place. Everybody knew each other, nobody locked their doors, and every mom looked after everybody else's kids. I was the oldest of five children and the first of my family to graduate from college. I know we weren't wealthy, but it never seemed that way. I held some kind of job from age nine or ten through my college years. Each job taught me something new about people and money. I shoveled snow (in that part of the country you could do this almost six months a year), I was a caddie, I bagged groceries, I worked at a ski area (as a lift attendant and ski instructor), I worked for the local Department of Public Works (I learned a lot about people and money there), and I even worked in a metal fabrication factory.

In high school I was a fairly good student-athlete. Well, maybe a better athlete than a student; regardless, I was accepted to Colgate University. Colgate broadened my perspective of people and money. I learned about economics, psychology, sociology, and philosophy. I learned to think and to look at the world from different points of view. I learned that people with money did, in fact, act differently than people who did not have money. I learned that it cost more to go on a weekend ski trip or fraternity road trip than it used to cost me to go to the movies in high school. I learned teaching skiing that sometimes it cost more for the gas to drive to the slope than I made teaching a ski class. What I really learned was that the economic theory I learned in class worked differently in the real world—behavior seemed to matter.

Toward the end of my freshman year, I made the most significant career decision of my life. I decided to join the Marine Corps. The recruiting officer made a great pitch. He said I could get in shape for football, earn a little money, and be just like John Wayne. That sounded like a good idea to me. I wanted to get out of New York State (you have to spend a few winters in Hamilton, NY, to appreciate what this means). I was up for the adventure, and I thought it would be a good way to get some money for graduate school.

I joined the Marine Corps Platoon Leaders' Course (PLC). It fit my style. I attended "boot camp" in the summer, which meant no drill or uniforms during the school year and a few extra dollars for books. All I needed to do was maintain a 2.0 grade-point average to be commissioned (it's good to have goals). I met my goal, and in the process helped a number of my classmates finish in the top half of our class. I was commissioned a Second Lieutenant of Marines just before graduation in 1973 and was the only member of my class to show up at graduation in a dress white uniform. In July I was off to Quantico, VA, for training. As it turned out, I was good at being a Marine. It also helped that I liked it. Life was good. I had a new car, a 14-inch color TV, and money in my pocket. At Quantico I had my first inkling that money did, in fact, make people crazy—me included.

Being a Marine 2Lt was the first real job most of us had ever had. It was also the first time any of us had "real" money, and we spent it accordingly. Most of us bought new cars right after commissioning. Looking back, I realize that I really did not think this through. I thought my 1974 Plymouth Duster was a great investment. It only cost me $109 a month for three years. I had a three-year commitment to the Marine Corps, so this was a no-brainer. But in the emotion of buying a new car, I failed to consider the cost of insurance and monthly living expenses, like uniforms, eating, partying, and getting engaged. I also didn't consider the fact that most Marines are sent to places where you either don't need or can't use a car. I was only one of a couple of hundred Lieutenants who had done the same thing. It turned out that I finished in the top of my class, and I selected Hawaii as my first duty station. Unfortunately, there was a bit of a gas shortage that summer. So I sold the car; actually, my dad sold the car, because I had to get to Ft. Sill, OK, for artillery school. I wonder where that car is now. What do you think its true cost was?

I survived being a Second Lieutenant and eventually got my financial house in order—retiring as a Lieutenant Colonel with 20-plus years of service. The Marine Corps taught me about people and money.

While on active duty I earned two master's degrees and served in a number of different assignments. In every assignment at every duty station I learned that human nature influences how people think and feel about money. The majority of the disciplinary problems I faced with my Marines—regardless of rank—were related to bad money choices. Too much debt was the biggest issue, followed by just a general misunderstanding of financial products and services. The result was poor job performance, lost productivity, divorce, domestic violence, substance abuse, loss of security clearances, and poor retention. I had Marines who wanted to retire or leave active duty, but due to their financial situation they could not afford to. They had to accept orders to move to places they did not want to go, to do things they did not want to do, with people they did not want to be with. Not the kind of situation anybody would want to be in.

Each assignment help develop my perception of people and money. In Hawaii I learned that self-preservation and taking care of your family is a strong emotional need. Hawaii is an expensive place to live. Very beautiful, but paradise is pricy. Many Marines—especially junior Marines and junior officers—could not afford to support their families due to the high cost of living on the island of Oahu. They always made money decisions to provide food and safety for their family—regardless of the inconvenience or stigma. This might mean living in a tent on the beach or sharing an apartment with one or more families. You don't need much of an imagination to envision how some of these decisions played out. Basic human needs are important and are taken care of first.

I taught economics at the United States Naval Academy for about three years. The courses, I thought, were all traditional economic theory classes. The assumption was that money decisions were made rationally. However, it became very obvious to me very quickly that the rational behavior we talked about in class was not the same behavior we witnessed outside of class. Let me give you an example:

Midshipmen are some of the brightest young men and women in the United States. Most have a very strong math/science background. You would think that these young men and women would be predisposed to act rationally. Not so; in fact, with the right incentive or stimulant, Midshipmen, who have IQs that are off the charts, can be just as stupid about money as the rest of us. Their money issues are just more complicated and thoughtful. Academy graduates must serve at least five years on active duty after graduation. That is an eternity to young men and women. Remember, these very bright young people spend four years "locked up" attending college while their peers are experiencing college at a civilian school. We had a number of newly commissioned officers who got into financial problems trying to cram a four-year college experience into the 90 days between graduation and reporting to their first duty station. The worst case I dealt with was a Second Lieutenant who in 90 days incurred over $67,000 in signature loans. He could not afford the payments on the loans. He ended up losing his commission and having to spend five years at sea as an enlisted Petty Officer. Just one example; I have more.

Just before Desert Storm, I was given the opportunity to apply the theory I learned from my MA in Instructional and Performance technology at Quantico. I ran the Marine Corps' Performance Technology Branch. Here we focused on training systems, human factors, performance, and behavior. We learned how important systems theory is to performance and how to design and implement performance systems. It worked during Desert Storm, and it works with money.

Before I retired I was the Aide to the Assistant Secretary of the Navy for Financial Management in Washington, DC. In that position we oversaw the financial management issues of the United States Navy and the United States Marine Corps. Since everything in the Department of Defense costs money, we were involved in everything everywhere. I observed that many of the same behaviors people showed with their own money could be seen when they worked on budgets and related finance issues. In other words, the way people think and feel about their own money also influences how they think and feel about other people's money—

budgets, purchases, pay, incentives, etc. It seems behavior matters more than we thought.

I started my career as a financial advisor about six months after retiring from the Marine Corps. I received very traditional financial services training—I was trained as a sales guy. I learned about the features and benefits of all kinds of financial products and services. I learned how to develop rapport and identify needs and sell stuff to meet those needs. My performance was measured by achieving sales goals, and I was rewarded accordingly. It turns out that I was very good at this. In fact, within a very short period of time I was one of the top producers in the company. I led the company in new clients and in the sale of one of our mutual funds. I was so good, in fact, that within a few years I was moved to the dark side—I became a manager.

I learned a great deal as a selling financial advisor. I learned that most of the people I worked with were good, honest folks who were following the American dream. I learned that the majority of the people I worked with either did not know very much about money or were not very good at managing money, regardless of what they knew. They looked to me to coach them.

As a manager, I spent most of my time working with advisors and less time working with clients. Growing a business, recruiting, and training became my number one focus. Although I worked with a lot of dedicated professionals, I began to question the traditional financial services sales model. It seemed we were training people to be very good at selling stuff but not very good at taking care of our clients' total financial needs. This bothered me. I began to look for an alternative approach. I wanted to see if anything I had learned in the Marne Corps about behavior and human performance could be applied to the financial services industry.

I also learned that financial advisors and clients behave the same way when it comes to money. The only difference is that advisors have more technical knowledge and access to a lot more information. However, they make the same mistakes. Advisors are human, and they will always behave just like you. This means that financial advisors also have a money temperament. The danger here is two-fold: An advisor's money temperament not only influences how they work with their own money, but it also influences how they work with you and your money.

During this period of self-examination, I became a student of neuroeconomics, behavioral economics, and behavioral finance. I read everything I could find on the subject. I'm hooked.

I've learned that behavior matters because we are human and will always act human. As a result, all of our decisions about money are about us. We are emotional and money decisions are emotional—even the thinking ones. We are uniquely imperfect.

The behaviors that perpetuate the species and keep us alive don't necessarily work all that well in a modern economy. This leads to issues between us and our money. The challenge is to figure out your money temperament—how you think and feel about money. Then, once you know your relationship with money, you can make better money decisions. Therefore, your goal is to understand and manage your money temperament, but not necessarily to change your money temperament. Very few people are so dysfunctional with money that they need professional clinical help. Most people simply need to find a fit between their money temperament, their money knowledge, their money strategy, and their money action plan.

That's what I hope to have accomplished with this book.

Lastly, writing this book has helped me link my Marine Corps experience with my financial advisor experience. This has caused a significant "I get it" moment for me. As a Marine I was trained: 1) to accomplish the mission—get the job done, 2) to take care of my Marines; and, 3) that officers eat last. This evolved into my personal philosophy of:

- Having an open mind—you can always learn something from everyone you meet.
- Having a sense of humor—never get to the point that you cannot laugh at yourself or your situation.
- Treating everyone with dignity—every human being has worth; look for it and embrace it.

This is how I run my business, Apexx Behavioral Solutions Group. This is how I treat my clients. This is how I treat my associates. This is also how I expect to treat you. Oh, and remember, at the end of the day, *money still makes me crazy and sometimes stupid.* And it always will—because I'm human, just like you.